What O
Anton Flore

These words come from friends, theologians, activists, and Casa Alterna guests—each a witness to the spirit of welcome, solidarity, and sacred story-sharing that fills these pages.

Voices of Faith and Justice

"God works through the cracks in everything. This is a book about community, tragedy, resilience, and defiant hope. I've been friends with Anton for over two decades, and he is a gift to the world. His courage and faith continue to inspire me. I'm so grateful he wrote this book—it reminds us that even when the devil tries to bury us, we are seeds. And we will rise."
— **Shane Claiborne**, author, activist, and co-founder of Red Letter Christians

"Welcome, Friends is more than a memoir—it is liturgy, lament, and a love letter. Through graceful storytelling, it sings a quiet hymn of hope, offering a transformative vision of friendship rooted in vulnerability and presence. These are not stories of 'moving on,' but of 'moving with.' On every page, readers will find themselves drawn into a deeper, more compassionate way of being—with one another and with God."
— **Sarah Jackson**, author of *The House That Love Built*

"When Anton Flores-Maisonet says, 'welcome,' he means it. In story, in poetry, in prayer, in life, Flores-Maisonet embodies radical hospitality that moves toward the power of shared vulnerability. If you're not already broken, this book will break you. If you are broken—and all of us are—you'll find in Welcome, Friends a refuge for sorrows and sustenance for the journey."
— **Kyle B.T. Lambelet**, Associate Professor at Virginia Theological Seminary and author of ¡*Presente!*

"Anton Flores-Maisonet is someone I always want to listen to and learn from because his words flow from a life deeply committed to faithful hospitality. He exudes authenticity, and Welcome, Friends is a sacred invitation to join a life of welcome, to listen deeply, and to leave changed."
— **Sarah Quezada**, author of *Love Undocumented*

"Anton Flores-Maisonet's work shows us what it means to be genuine vessels of divine love in a broken world. He embraces the messiness of life while remaining steadfastly committed to a vision of radical hospitality where all are welcomed and embraced and where everyone's voice matters. He is humble, wise, and prophetic. Welcome, Friends is a gift, and one the world very much needs now."
— **Christina Repoley**, Vice President of Program, Forum for Theological Exploration

Voices of Casa Alterna

"I want to express my heartfelt gratitude for the unconditional support of Casa Alterna and everyone who lives there. Together, we became like a small family."
— **Yohelena**, Casa Alterna resident

"When I first arrived in the U.S., I was scared and without a place to call home. But Casa Alterna embraced me with peace, family, and love. They showed me that life is about sharing with those in need and giving generously to others."
— **Erylyn**, Casa Alterna resident

"My family is deeply grateful for all that Casa Alterna has done for us. Your support and kindness go beyond words, and your steadfast dedication to helping others inspires us as we begin this new chapter in this beautiful country."
— **Ana María**, Casa Alterna guest

WELCOME, FRIENDS

Stories of hope and hospitality with immigrants

Eva & Rob,
Love crosses borders. Keep following love.
Anton

WELCOME, FRIENDS

Stories of hope and hospitality with immigrants

ANTON FLORES-MAISONET

Story Sanctum
PUBLISHING

Copyright © 2025 by Anton Flores-Maisonet.

All rights reserved. No part of this book may be used or reproduced in any form whatsoever without written permission except in the case of brief quotations in critical articles or reviews.

Cover image: Casselberry Creative Design via Wix AI Image Creator.

Cover design and interior formatting provided by Casselberry Creative Design.

Story Sanctum Publishing, LLC

ISBN: 979-8-9928559-3-7

Eli, now we are both authors

TABLE OF CONTENTS

A Word Before You Begin   13
Prologue: Touch My Wounds   15

JULY 2019 - FEBRUARY 2020

Recalculating: The Grace of Transition   21
Becoming Sanctuary   25

PANDEMIC 2020

Hope in the Time of Pandemic   31
God Has Left the Building   33
The Stranger   37
Praying with Our Feet   39
Because I'm Happy   43
Where the Heart Already Was   47
Yes, Please   51
Under the Canopy   55
Oooo, My Favorite   59

2021

A Hopeful, Hard, and Happy New Year   65
No Place to Go   69
When the Van Turns Back   71
Su Casa es Su Casa   75
A Mother Holds On   79
The Grit of Life   83
Joy Took the Wheel   85
Béni's Attitude   89
Surely, God is With Us   93

2022 - 2024

One Long Journey	99
The Gift of a Mirror	103
On Prophets and "Pastorcitos"	107
Crisis or Community?	111
They Carry Hope	115
Beloved and Cradled	119
The Welcome Table	123
The Quinceañera and the One-Armed Companion	127
The Border-Crossing Power of Love	131
A Sanctuary of Love	137
Beloved Strength: Welcoming New Life and Resilience	141
Antonella's Journey	145

MARCH TO JUNE 2024

This Is My Broken Body	151
Find a Way Home	155

TRUMP 2.0

Ending Political Violence Begins with Welcome	161
Radical Hospitality as Resistance	165
Midwives of Justice: A Call for Sanctuary	169
No Way Back Home	173
Love is the Way Home	179
Defiant Thanks at the Gates	183
Standing in Love, Not Fear	187
Beloved, Not Exceptional	191
Mary, Don't You Weep	195
Compas at the Gates	201

Epilogue: Carry On, The Welcome Never Ends	205

A Word Before You Begin

Welcome, Friends holds stories of deep grief, loss, trauma, and resilience. It includes reflections on suicide, mental illness, immigration hardships, detention, and the complex realities faced by asylum seekers and immigrants.

Readers may find some passages emotionally intense or triggering. Please care for yourself as you read. You are invited to approach these stories at your own pace and to seek support if needed.

If you or someone you know is struggling, help is available. You can reach the Suicide & Crisis Lifeline by calling or texting 988 anytime.

Whether the moral arc of the universe bends toward justice on its own or because it is our duty to bend it, I trust that hope is the overarching message of this book. Amid stories of grief and struggle, may you find courage, compassion, and the call to radical hospitality as pathways toward a more beautiful world.

Prologue: Touch My Wounds

It wasn't just Eli.

The week my 14-year-old son died by suicide—his brilliant mind overtaken by psychosis—our co-founder Norma also passed away. Norma had lived in our intentional community for 14 years. She died with the same fierce dignity with which she had lived, after a long journey with end-stage renal disease. Her body failed her slowly; Eli's mind betrayed him suddenly. Both lived and died within our embrace.

The searing loss from that week carved a hollow so deep that I wasn't sure I'd ever find my way out. For months, I lay in bed, wrapped in the darkness of grief. Yet healing sometimes comes not through escape, but by returning to the practice of presence, the sacredness of community, and the balm of hospitality. We moved to Mona Lane, a small cul-de-sac in LaGrange, home to about 25 immigrant families. In that sea of children—nearly 50 spilling joyfully into the narrow street—I heard echoes of Eli's laughter and purpose. We organized a food co-op, launched youth initiatives, and improved housing and neighborhood conditions. I became a community leader again—this time, one with wounds—and my neighbors, hailing from distant lands, met me with the kind of grace our nation had denied them. They welcomed me with warm empathy and even warmer empanadas.

Vulnerability is at the core of hospitality. Without it, we fear the stranger, build walls, and demonize difference. However, healthy vulnerability, like Christ entering the Upper Room bearing his wounds, is an act of healing. The risen Jesus does not hide his scars. He offers them, saying, "Peace. Touch my wounds." In my woundedness, I have tried to do the same. Through my vulnerability, I hope to be a vessel of peace.

In 2019, Charlotte and I left LaGrange after many years of living in an intentional community we founded with our adopted Latin American family. We relocated to metro Atlanta for healing, to be closer to Jairo, our oldest son, and to enter a new phase of discernment as empty nesters. That move ushered in another chapter of radical welcome, this time shaped by a pandemic and the Quaker witness of peace, simplicity, and equality. What began as a two-year residency as Friend-in-Residence with the Atlanta Friends Meeting has now become an open-ended collaboration between Quakers and Casa Alterna.

In the past five years, nearly 600 asylum seekers from over 50 countries have found refuge inside the meetinghouse through this ministry of hospitality I launched and continue to nurture. What once seemed impossible—a congregation opening its physical space to house strangers —has become a rhythm of grace. A sojourner enters, not as a client or guest, but as a Friend. The Meeting's greeting— "Welcome, Friends"—is more than liturgical politeness; it is a radical statement rooted in the belief that there is that of God in everyone.

These overlapping circles have shaped my life: the broken circle of grief, the nurturing circle of community, the welcoming circle of hospitality, and the eternal circle of God's transforming love. Each circle overlaps at the point of vulnerability. It is the place of touch—the place of scars—and the beginning of resurrection.

Welcome, Friends is not just a memoir. It is a testimony. It is my way of saying that hope still lives, even when everything else breaks. It is also a hymn of gratitude for the friends who have walked with me, welcomed me, and taught me to do the same.

At the end of each chapter, you will find a question titled "At the Threshold." These reflections invite you to pause and enter into the space of vulnerability and welcome— those liminal moments when we meet the stranger, bear our wounds, or open ourselves to transformation. Each question is a threshold, an invitation to stand at the edge of the story and consider how radical hospitality might touch your own life. My hope is that these moments of reflection will invite you, dear friend, into a deeper participation in the work of welcome and the healing power of presence.

JULY 2019 - FEBRUARY 2020
Drawn By The Silence

Charlotte and I arrive at the Atlanta Friends Meeting to begin a two-year commitment as Friend-in-Residence. It's been three years since our son Eli died, and with Jairo now off at college, we are drawn here by a quiet yearning—for stillness, for discernment, for renewal in our life, ministry, and marriage.

The world outside is, for the moment, unshaken. No one yet speaks of global pandemics or lockdowns. But beneath the surface, something is stirring. We feel it in ourselves, in the hush of worship, in the rhythms of this meetinghouse. A kind of hopeful tremor. A question rising from the silence: What if life could be more beautiful than we've dared imagine?

Recalculating: The Grace of Transition

How beautiful can life be? We hardly dare imagine it.
—Charles Eisenstein

Just below the meetinghouse, commuter trains rumble steadily—like a heartbeat beneath the surface. I feel in that steady pulse the rumblings of Spirit. It's a hopeful tremor, what Charles Eisenstein calls "the more beautiful world our hearts know is possible." That possibility feels close, almost urgent.

In my brief time as Friend in Residence here at the Atlanta Friends Meeting, I have found myself drawn into the quiet rhythm of contemplation and action that hums through this place every day. From worship to First Day School, from shared meals with newcomers to friendly conversations, I am learning the patterns of a community rooted in peace and welcome.

I've witnessed hospitality in many forms: in gentle

greetings, in the care extended to those who gather here, and in the spaces we create for one another. This meetinghouse is more than a building—it is a threshold where lives intersect: seen and unseen, known and unknown.

The presence of people like Dieudonne, our custodian, reveals that sacredness even in the stillest hours. Often before dawn, I hear the soft sounds of his work, steady and faithful. His name means "God has given," and truly, God has given me a gift in witnessing his humble dedication. His presence is a quiet testimony to the grace that holds this community.

There is Constance, the crossing guard I pass by when I ride my bike. Her watchful care for the neighborhood's children, the gentle reminders she offers, all speak of the quiet ways love shows up in public life—unassuming but essential.

After hours, the meetinghouse falls into a holy stillness. The trains passing nearby mark time like monastic bells, their distant rumble to me like the groanings of a more beautiful world trying to emerge.

Yet this call to hospitality and peace feels wrapped in transition.

Not long ago, my GPS sent me on an unexpected detour through Lullwater Preserve. Few people were there. The landscape was simple, gracious, inviting calm. The voice of my old GPS, steady and patient, has stayed with me—not scolding, only saying: "Recalculating."

Transitions are like that—times to pause, to reorient. Every ending carries a new beginning.

If you find yourself navigating change after years

of familiar ground, I offer three guiding points, like GPS coordinates for the journey ahead:

Grace.
Transitions rarely come with clear instructions. When Thomas asked Jesus, "How can we know the way?" Jesus said, "I am the way." The way of Jesus is the way of grace. Be gentle with others who are slow to catch your vision. Be gentle with yourself when you stumble or fall short. Hospitality is rooted in graciousness—not perfection.

People.
We are not meant to walk alone. In a fractured world, embodied community—around tables, in worship, on porches—keeps us human. Transitions call us to say goodbye to some relationships and welcome new ones. Step away from the curated nostalgia of social media. Ahead lies a vista more breathtaking than the one behind.

Simplicity.
Simplicity is not minimalism, but clarity. It is knowing what matters most, then choosing accordingly. The freedom simplicity brings can ease the anxiety that change often stirs. Name your core values. Let them guide how you say "yes" and "no." Make room for rest. Lay down what no longer serves your life.

Transitions are sacred thresholds, even when uncomfortable. Let grace, people, and simplicity be your companions. And when you stray, as we all do, listen closely for that still, small voice—the Spirit whispering, "Recalculating."

At the Threshold
In seasons of transition, what helps you stay grounded in grace, connected to people, and clear about what truly matters?

Becoming Sanctuary

Sometimes we are called to prepare a place before we know exactly for whom or for what.

"What do you do?" someone at Atlanta Friends Meeting asked me not long after I arrived.

It's a question that often passes as small talk, but in this season of my life, it landed with unexpected weight. How could I explain what I was doing when so much of me still felt undone—displaced, discerning, uncertain, and in between?

My wife, Charlotte, and I had recently moved into the Friend-in-Residence apartment at the meetinghouse. We carried with us more questions than answers, more longing than clarity. We had left behind a fuller household, a known community, and stepped into something quieter, simpler, and unfamiliar. I was learning how to welcome myself here.

But even in that in-between time, something was

stirring.

I pedaled my old mountain bike along narrow streets and wooded trails, winding through Decatur, Clarkston, and Atlanta. It became a kind of contemplative practice, one rotation of the wheels at a time. Charlotte walked to and from school most days, often bringing home stories from her classroom and her long, reflective stroll from Medlock Park to the meetinghouse. Our shared shift away from constant car travel—toward public transportation, walking, biking—became more than a logistical choice. It felt like a realignment. Our bodies, our budget, our spirits, even our carbon footprint—all were gently invited into new rhythms.

Inside the meetinghouse, I began collaborating with Kevin, the new property coordinator, to explore how this space might more fully reflect Quaker values of simplicity, peace, integrity, community, equality, and care for the earth. These weren't just lofty ideals—they were invitations to root ourselves in practice.

I also began dipping my toes into gentle acts of accompaniment—helping with asylum defense workshops in partnership with Innovation Law Lab, offering rides, welcoming Central American guests. At that stage, it was less about leadership and more about listening. Less about fixing and more about showing up. The "doing" was humble: open a door, drive across town, share a meal.

One night, I welcomed a Cuban man named Humberto, recently released from immigration detention. He was kind-eyed and weary. After years of journeying and months of detention—months apart from his wife, Ana— he walked into the meetinghouse and tasted freedom for the first time in the U.S. We ate pizza and watched the World Series. The next morning, I helped him catch a bus to reunite with Ana in Texas. This was the first night the meetinghouse would be a new kind of sanctuary.

At the same time, I was connecting with others—like Presencia, a local organization supporting immigrant youth. Their leadership team came to the meetinghouse one evening, gathering in the backyard, sharing a meal in our apartment, and reflecting on the meaning of Beloved Community. In a room full of teenagers dreaming of justice, I felt something awaken.

Charlotte's school, the International Community School, was another spark. Over 400 students, 25 languages, 30 nationalities. When she told me the school was opening a Community Resource Center, I offered to help. We began collecting food, hygiene supplies, multilingual books. It wasn't glamorous—but it was grounding.

And there were lighter moments too. Charlotte and I started a weekly trivia team at Mellow Mushroom—a small, joyful ritual that combined her love of pizza, my love of games, and our shared desire to root friendship into our week. We hosted newcomer dinners for those exploring the Quaker tradition. Community was forming, gently and quietly.

So—what did I do?

I biked. I shared pizza. I showed up. I played trivia. I planted seeds I hoped would grow.

What I was really doing was learning to dwell in the unknown—trusting that welcome must begin with presence, that discernment is often slow, and that hospitality, like faith, starts before the door is ever knocked upon.

In those early days at the meetinghouse, I didn't yet know the fullness of what this place would become. But I was beginning to glimpse it: a sanctuary rising not from perfection, but from intention—from everyday acts of connection, courage, and quiet hope.

In the ordinary rhythms of that season—in displacement, in discernment, and in presence—I found the sacred showing up again and again.

At the Threshold
In seasons when you feel uprooted or unsure, how might you stay present, make space for others, and trust that even in uncertainty, the seeds of hospitality can begin to grow?

PANDEMIC 2020
Prelude to Hope

In March 2020, as the world closed its doors and the streets fell silent, so too did our meetinghouse. A space once alive with song, laughter, prayer, and protest now echoed only with the occasional creaks of its wooden benches and the rumble of subway train running directly below us. Charlotte and I were alone. The stillness was surprisingly comforting.

What I didn't yet know was that the silence had something to teach me.

In the hush of that early pandemic solitude, I began to hear a different kind of worship. Not one of hymns or preaching, but the quiet pulse of presence. The spaciousness of unknowing. A holy hush that asked not for homilies, but for listening. It was as if the walls themselves were breathing, waiting for something to be born.

At first, I could only sit. And listen. And write.

The Spirit was already at work, though her whispers were

barely audible. What felt like a pause was, in truth, a preparation—a gestation. A Way was opening, not through the clamor of certainty but through the trembling quiet of vulnerability. I didn't know then that the emptiness would soon make room for something sacred: the arrival of weary travelers seeking rest, the birth of a new rhythm of welcome, the reshaping of our lives around love.

Hope was beginning to stir.

Even now, I remember that moment—those first days of disorientation and stillness—and I understand them differently. What I once experienced as loss, I now know was invitation.

Hope, I've learned, is not always loud. Sometimes it sounds like sparrows outside the window. Sometimes it echoes like memory in an empty sanctuary. Sometimes it is silence that prepares us for resurrection.

Hope in the Time of Pandemic

I sit
in silence
in this sanctuary;
the sounds
of sniffles
make me suspicious.

Beneath
the busy-ness
of my brain,
the beat,
or beats,
of my heart beckon.

The sound
of sparrows
outside this space,

all sing,
all say,
Hope is an eternal spring.

At the Threshold
Where or how do you find hope during times of fear and uncertainty?

God Has Left the Building
Finding Resurrection and Solidarity in a Time of Isolation

Recently, a friend asked me, "How's the 'God business' these days?"

I replied with a bit of humor, borrowing from an old Elvis catchphrase: "God has left the building."

I live inside a Quaker meetinghouse, closed due to the COVID-19 pandemic. Worship has moved to video conferences, and our physical sacred space is momentarily empty. But my playful comment lingered in my mind and invited me to reflect on the deeper meaning of saying, "God has left the building."

George Fox, the founder of Quakerism, urged us to "walk cheerfully over the world, answering that of God in everyone." Even though Easter services are canceled and the world seems to be in lockdown, this invitation remains: we are called to roll away the stones of our own limitations and step into new life. Resurrection and hope are possible, even amid uncertainty.

But how do we walk cheerfully into a world that is physically closed off? How can we answer that of God in everyone when we are asked to stay apart?

Here are some thoughts I've found helpful as I try to live into those questions:

Be a Monastic in This New Time
During this season of the novel coronavirus, contemplative and monastic traditions remind us that solitude can be sacred. Instead of feeling confined, consider turning your home into a cloister—a place set apart for intimacy with God. Carve out times for unplugged silence and prayer. Share honestly with God what is on your heart. And if you are sheltering with others, discover new ways to create face-to-face community, even if it's through a screen.

Be a Vulnerable Priest
Like many, I have felt anxiety and fear over my inability to protect loved ones. But I have learned that love, not fear, is the antidote. When I show up as my true self, I find a vulnerable priest inside who offers words of peace and invites others to share their wounds, just as I share mine. These days, I regularly check in with friends who live alone or who may be at higher risk if they get sick. Simple phone calls, video chats, or written notes become meaningful ways to practice mutuality, vulnerability, and connectedness.

Be a Prophetic Voice
For seventeen years, I have lived in community and solidarity

with immigrants. I have witnessed their hardships, heard their cries, and known their resilience. Immigrants remind me that God's Beloved Community, more powerful than any virus, is a cure that knows no borders. Their witness compels me to raise my voice for a more just and beautiful world. During this pandemic, I have leaned into social media and video conferencing to draw public attention to immigrants in detention. I am also creating circles of solidarity and mutual aid, like a recent campaign to assist a single immigrant mother who is unemployed and without a social safety net. Who are the most vulnerable among us who stand to lose the most as health and economic systems strain? How can you stand in solidarity with them, even now?

God has left the building, not out of fear or retreat, but because God's work is happening beyond these walls. Easter is not canceled. A world awaits resurrection and new life.

At the Threshold
How might you turn solitude into a sacred space, offer vulnerability as a way to connect, and raise your voice in prophetic witness—even when the world feels closed off?

The Stranger

What we fear is the stranger—
How sadly this word harmonizes with danger.
What is this fear of others?
Is it a projection of a self we despise?
What we fear is the stranger—
How sadly this word harmonizes with danger.

What we follow are distractions—
How easily the world rewards half-hearted action.
What is this fable called the rat race?
Is it the fallacy of self-sufficiency that keeps us in debt?
What we follow are distractions—
How easily the world rewards half-hearted action.

What we fear is the stranger within—
How unsettling to meet the one beneath our skin.
What if we simply said hello?

Is loving ourselves a kind of death?
What we fear is the stranger within—
How unsettling to meet the one beneath our skin.

At the Threshold
How might you face the fear of the stranger—both in others and within yourself—and choose connection over distance?

Praying with Our Feet

In memory of Santiago Baten-Oxlaj, who died of COVID-19 on May 25, 2020, while in ICE custody at Stewart Detention Center.

Since 2007, I have joined with immigrants, allies, and organizations to call for the closure of Stewart Detention Center—a 1,900-bed private immigration facility in southwest Georgia. During the COVID-19 pandemic, our coalition, including Georgia Detention Watch and others, renewed our calls with urgency. We urged federal and state authorities to shut down this overcrowded facility in the name of public health. Our pleas were ignored.

We appealed to the Stewart County Commission to act for the well-being of its community. Even as they continued to receive federal funds for each person imprisoned—including Santiago Baten-Oxlaj—they refused to pass even a symbolic resolution calling for closure.

Southwest Georgia became a COVID-19 hotspot. Stewart reported more guards infected with the virus than any jail or prison in the state. The pandemic laid bare the deadly consequences of locking vulnerable people in unsafe, crowded conditions.

Frederick Douglass once said, "Praying for freedom never did me any good until I started praying with my feet." That line took on new meaning for me in those pandemic months. Masked and distanced, I tried to embody that call—to show up for those most at risk from both the virus and the systems of injustice that allowed it to flourish.

I joined Black Lives Matter protests in downtown Atlanta and on Auburn Avenue, and stood in silent vigils with Mennonite friends in East Atlanta. At the same time, we continued accompanying migrants released from Stewart and dropped off at the Atlanta airport—often with no warning, no plan, and no support. Since the start of the pandemic, we've helped more than fifty people: printing boarding passes, navigating terminals, offering meals and basic supplies. Our local team and the remote volunteers at Paz Amigos made this possible.

One man especially stays with me. Still recovering from COVID-19, he was suddenly released by ICE with no notice and left alone at the airport—disoriented, exhausted, and without connections. A volunteer couple welcomed him into their home for several weeks. Soon, I'll accompany him to another hospitality ministry, where he'll stay until he can return safely to his home country.

The fight to shut down Stewart and protect the dignity

of detained immigrants is far from over. But in the midst of this struggle, the courage of families, communities, and advocates continues to shine. They welcome the stranger, even when institutions detain or discard them. Their love and resistance are reminders that even in the darkest of times, another way is possible.

At the Threshold
When the world is hurting and justice delayed, how might you pray with your feet?

Because I'm Happy

I met Omar not long after he was released from immigration detention. He had crossed borders and oceans, continents and danger zones—traversing the Horn of Africa, the Middle East, South and Central America, and finally Mexico. His journey was not the stuff of headlines, though it could have been. It was the kind of quiet epic known mostly to those who survive it.

The officials at the detention center had dropped him off at the Atlanta airport too late to catch his connecting flight to the West Coast, where a relative—someone he had never met in person—was waiting for him. So Omar needed somewhere to sleep. That's how he ended up with us: a few Quakers, some casseroles in the freezer, and a mattress in a quiet guest room.

After everything—after sleeping in forests and bus terminals, crossing the Darién Gap on foot, and losing contact for weeks with his brother, who remained detained in another state—one might expect exhaustion or bitterness to settle in. But instead, Omar turned to me, eyes crinkling above his mask, and said, "Allah must have a reason why I get to spend time with you. And for that, I am happy."

There it was: joy.

Not a naïve joy. Not denial. But something deeper. An offering of trust. A declaration of dignity. A quiet resistance to despair.

Later that evening, I offered to take him out for a meal. We walked through our neighborhood, and I listed some of the options in our little foodie town: samosas and dal, pad thai and curry, crepes and baguettes, enchiladas and tamales, or good old Southern fried chicken.

"And of course," I added, "there's always American fast food."

Guess which one he chose?

He had never been to that particular chain before, but something about it symbolized America—and that called to him. He ordered chicken nuggets and fries.

When the cashier asked what sauce he wanted, he hesitated, unsure. I explained to her that it was his first time ever inside this famous chain and asked if we could try all the sauces. I even offered to pay extra.

The manager overheard and interrupted with a smile: "Let them have the sauce—on the house."

It felt like a small gesture. But I've come to believe there are no small gestures, especially when dignity is on the line.

We took our food to a quiet picnic table and ate under the night sky. Between bites, Omar began to share: six years without electricity. Sleepless nights in a country marred by war. The decision to flee made in whispers. His story stretched across cultures and languages—interwoven with people from Haiti, Iran, and the margins of maps. Each chapter bore the weight of loss, and yet here he was: tasting new food, savoring every sauce, present and alive.

The next morning, we left before sunrise. Before we departed, he prayed—folding his body in reverence while the rest of the house still slept. In the car, windows cracked and masks on, I asked what kind of music he liked. I played a few Arabic songs from my collection, but he shook his head gently.

"American pop," he said, smiling. "That's how I learned English."

So I switched to a local station. Pharrell Williams' "Happy" came on.

Omar lit up. "Oh, I love this song!"

And then, softly, he sang along:

Because I'm happy
Clap along if you feel like a room without a roof...
Because I'm happy
Clap along if you feel like happiness is the truth...
Because I'm happy
Clap along if you know what happiness is to you...
Because I'm happy
Clap along if you feel like that's what you wanna do...

That joy again. Not the kind sold in commercials, but the kind forged through suffering, carried with reverence, and offered as a gift.

He was on his way to build a life with someone whose name he'd only seen in text. His brother remained behind bars, and his own future was far from certain.

And yet—he was happy.

I carry Omar's voice with me. His hope, his resilience, his light. And I keep a copy of that song on my phone—because sometimes, we need to remember what joy sounds like after exile.

At the Threshold
In your own journey, when has joy become an act of resistance?

Where the Heart Already Was

Mario is a high school student, but this is not a story about first days or last bells. It is about belonging—the kind that isn't granted by paperwork or performance, but by love and accompaniment.

A few years ago, Mario made the long and dangerous journey from Central America to the United States. He came alone. By the time I met him, he was a varsity athlete with one year left before graduation—quiet, determined, and deeply rooted in a school community that clearly valued him. He had a legal guardian—a U.S. citizen—in a Western state, someone officially designated to care for him. But that's not how the story unfolded.

The reason Mario was in Georgia, far from his school and teammates, wasn't because of a transfer or summer break. According to Mario—and confirmed by two of his teachers, both of whom I spoke with directly—his guardian had brought him to Georgia and placed him in the home of a relative, where he was forced to work. The labor was unpaid. The conditions were dehumanizing. After weeks of verbal and physical abuse, Mario fled and called the police.

When his teachers heard what had happened, they didn't hesitate. They reached across the miles to connect with local advocates here, and soon Mario found refuge with a family connected to the Georgia Latino Alliance for Human Rights. After a few days in their home, I was asked to meet with him and help discern the next steps.

He knew what he wanted. He didn't want to bounce from couch to couch or shelter to shelter. He didn't want to return to the one who had failed to protect him. What he longed for—what he called home—was his school. His team. His teachers. The coach who cheered him on and checked in when he limped after practice. The counselor who showed a genuine regard for his well-being. The classroom where he was called by his name and not by a file number.

That was where he felt seen. That was where he felt safe.

So we made a plan. His teachers advocated. The network around him held strong. He was aware of the risks—of traveling alone again, of the legal ambiguity still swirling around his case. But he was steady. Calm. Determined.

For two nights, our Quaker meetinghouse became his resting place. He didn't carry much—just a small school backpack with the essentials and a well-worn pair of sneakers. We didn't talk much about the trauma. Instead, we talked about what gave him joy: his teammates, math class, early morning jogs, and a particular dish his school cafeteria served on Fridays.

Before the sun rose, we stepped out into the stillness. We hugged goodbye, and he set off on a two-day journey—not toward something new, but back to what had already become home.

He made it. Safely.

His coach—one of the teachers who had advocated for him from the beginning—welcomed him not just onto the team or back into the classroom, but into their own home. Because the truth is, they had already made space for him in their heart.

That, to me, is the spirit of hospitality. Not simply opening a door, but recognizing another's longing for home—and responding with presence, accompaniment, and tenderness. Sometimes hospitality means creating room in our spare bedrooms or sanctuaries. But more often, it means expanding the heart to match the needs of another human being.

Mario didn't just return to a school. He returned to a community that had already claimed him as beloved.

At the Threshold
What does it mean for your heart to make room before your home ever does?

Yes, Please

When I asked Abdoulaye about his languages, he smiled and said, "I speak ten." Most were tribal tongues from his home in West Africa, each carrying its own rhythm and memory. His English was clear and steady, but what struck me was the way he spoke—a graceful insistence on kindness and humility, embodied in one phrase he repeated again and again: "Yes, please."

"Would you like something to drink?"
"Yes, please."
"Is this your first time in the United States?"
"Yes, please."

In English, this phrase isn't always necessary. Yet from him, it held a gentle dignity—a quiet thread of politeness woven through a language that was not his own. It felt like an offering, a doorway to connection, even amid all the unfamiliarity.

Abdoulaye's story unfolded slowly. He shared

his long journey—crossing borders, surviving the cruel conditions of detention, the relief of reuniting with his sister in a new place. His words carried a weight that demanded respect and silence in equal measure.

When I invited him to share about his decision to seek asylum, the pause that came before his answer was heavy. Then, with honesty that was both raw and brave, he said:

"Yes, please. I am homosexual. My partner and I were attacked. He was killed, and I had to flee."

How do you hold someone who carries such deep wounds? The loss of a beloved. The terror of persecution for simply being who they are. The exhaustion of running and hiding, crossing invisible borders of fear. The dehumanization inside detention centers, where suspicion replaces justice. The multiplying grief that follows every step.

In that moment, I wanted to wrap him in an embrace. But because of COVID, even touch was a risk. A new kind of wall had risen—made of fear and invisibility—that distanced us not only physically but emotionally.

So what could I offer?

A different kind of embrace.

One shaped by shared vulnerability.

Hospitality that honors presence without expectation.

A peaceful welcome that says, "You are seen. You are held. You are safe here."

Do I dream of a world where no one is imprisoned for seeking safety?

Yes, please.

Do I long for a day when queerness is met with celebration, not fear?

Yes, please.

Do I believe love can cross every border, dismantle every wall, and proclaim with certainty:

You are welcome here.

Yes, please.

At the Threshold
How might you offer a "yes, please" — a gentle, open welcome — to someone whose pain is difficult to witness?

Under the Canopy

"Hospitality is not to change people, but to offer them space where change can take place."
— Henri Nouwen

The winds blew gusty that day when Didier arrived at our door, freshly released from months of detention and months of waiting. Nine months confined in a place where hope often withers. His asylum was granted by a judge known for denying almost every case — a rare moment of justice amid an often cruel system.

Didier's release was not just a legal victory; it was a testament to perseverance, faith, and resilience. During the brief time he stayed with us, he shared something deeper than stories—he shared music, the powerful voice of Nigerian gospel singer Frank Edwards, whose song became a quiet anthem in our home:

Oh yes, you cover me

Under the canopy
Give me security
I am the righteousness of God

Hospitality is often thought of as a shelter we offer to those who arrive weary from long journeys—an act of giving refuge and safety. But Didier taught me that hospitality is not just a one-way gift. His strength, his courage, and his faith became a gift to us. In the shelter of our home, he offered something sacred: a reminder of how resilience is rooted in a love that holds us beyond all systems of cruelty.

Didier comes from a country gripped by violent conflict—where young people like him, students, teachers, lawyers, sought to raise their voices for justice. They were met with fire, torture, and silence. The government's brutal campaign was met in turn by armed groups bent on vengeance. Schools were attacked, villages razed, and lives shattered.

To survive, Didier fled—first across continents, through the perilous Darién Gap, a place so wild and lawless it tests every step of those who cross it. He traveled on, alone, through Central America and Mexico, finally arriving at a border that held him captive, stripped of freedom and the dignity of a fair chance.

And yet, through it all, Didier carried a song of hope:

Oh yes, you cover me
Under the canopy
Give me security
I am the righteousness of God

When governments fail, when borders dehumanize, when systems of power seek to define and diminish, Didier knew a greater truth. There is a canopy that shelters beyond any walls, a love that enfolds us as beloved children, righteous and whole.

I think of Didier whenever anxiety creeps in, whenever fear tries to silence the song within. I hum that simple chorus. And I dance—however awkwardly—under the canopy of grace.

At the Threshold
What does hospitality mean when it becomes a two-way exchange of strength, healing, and courage?

Oooo, My Favorite

It was the Winter Solstice, the longest night of the year. To mark it with light and warmth, Charlotte and I invited the refugee guests staying with us on a driving tour of holiday lights. We packed our vehicle with just enough room for a little interfaith caravan—Muslim and Christian, Spanish and Arabic and English, all bundled together in one moving sanctuary.

Before we pulled out of the parking lot of Atlanta Friends Meeting, I gave the three young boys riding with us—our wise ones from the East—a small invitation: "At the end of the drive, tell me which house had your favorite lights."

We turned on some soft instrumental holiday music, the kind that evokes nostalgia without demanding attention. As we crept along the neighborhood streets, the sounds from the stereo were quickly overtaken by something more beautiful: a rising chorus of exclamations from the backseat.

Wonder poured forth like water from a loosened faucet.

When I opened the moon roof so we could look up at the rare "Bethlehem Star"—a planetary alignment that hadn't graced the sky in 800 years—the boys' excitement was nearly explosive. For a moment, it felt like the night itself expanded to make room for their joy.

I had asked them to wait until the end to declare a favorite. But four-year-old Amin either didn't catch that part or didn't see the need for restraint. As soon as we passed the first home lit up in spectacular fashion, he yelled out, his whole body animated with joy: "Oooo, my favorite!"

Charlotte and I laughed. It was the first full phrase we'd heard him say since he and his family arrived three weeks earlier. And what a phrase to start with—not just a sentence, but a song. A proclamation. Joy, breaking through a long silence.

But Amin wasn't done.

Every new house that glowed with lights—no matter how grand or modest—received the same unfiltered, uncontainable response:

"Oooo, my favorite!"

"Oooo, my favorite!"

Over and over again.

That night, a four-year-old Muslim refugee child taught me one of the most important lessons of Christmas. And he did it not with scripture or tradition, but with presence.

This was during the pandemic, when many of us were distanced from the people and patterns that gave our lives texture and comfort. We were navigating grief, fear, and exhaustion. The world felt as if it were holding its breath.

But Amin wasn't looking back in mourning, nor forward in dread. He didn't linger on what we'd already passed. He didn't try to predict where we were going. He simply embraced the moment we were in, named its beauty, and rejoiced in it. Again and again.

No refugee family leaves home without heartbreak in their rearview mirror. The trauma that trails them is real. And the road ahead is often shadowed with uncertainty.

But on this longest of nights, it was a little boy who became a messenger of joy, peace, hope, and love. Not because all was well. But because he was fully awake to what was.

The present is a gift.
And if we open ourselves to it—
despite what has been lost,
despite what is unknown—
it just might be our favorite.

At the Threshold
What small steps can you take today to reclaim a wonder that dares to shout, "Oooo, my favorite"?

2021
Way Opens

As our two-year residency at Atlanta Friends Meeting draws to a close, it becomes clear—as Friends would say, that the Way has opened before us. A resurrected ministry of radical hospitality has been embraced wholeheartedly and is now held under the care of the Quaker Meeting. This emerging stability bears abundant fruit, and in its wake, we are invited to continue as Friends-in-Residence indefinitely.

Yet the path ahead remains both hopeful and hard, marked by new arrivals seeking refuge, the fragile joys of freedom, and the daunting challenges that follow release from detention. The flicker of light from this ministry is steady but calls us deeper into the work of sanctuary and accompaniment. In this liminal moment, we hold tightly to hope, knowing the journey ahead will demand courage, grace, and fierce love.

A Hopeful, Hard, and Happy New Year

We closed out 2020 with the living room full and the lights turned low. A mother and her three children from Southeast Asia, a woman from East Asia, and another from Eurasia gathered with us in that room of the meetinghouse—our little sanctuary carved out of the chaos of a long, hard year.

It had been a season of sorrow and strain—for the world, yes, but especially for these women. The two single women had been released just days earlier from Irwin County Detention Center, one of the most notorious immigration prisons in the country. That place, with its history of coercion, neglect, and medical abuse—particularly of women—had swallowed months of their lives. But now, they were free. They had been through fire. And still, they arrived with grace.

So, on New Year's Eve, we did something radical: we celebrated.

Some of our guests made pizza for the first time in

their lives—kneading dough, spreading sauce, laughing over toppings. We ate until we were full and made sure there was enough left over for the next day. Some of the children even discovered the joy of cold pizza for breakfast.

Later, we gathered in a large room with a projector and shared a movie together. By the time midnight approached, a few of us had already drifted off to sleep. Others stood quietly by the windows, watching fireworks burst across the night sky—temporary stars over a house full of fragile hope.

That hope would need to carry us into the coming year. One woman was set to travel the next morning to Jubilee Partners, a community that's been welcoming immigrants for decades. Another was headed to a large city in the Northeast, navigating it alone. Her future was unclear. No documents. No plan beyond the name of a shelter. The same government that had locked her up without cause had now released her without support. It made no sense. It rarely does.

Before she left, the woman going to Jubilee—nearly fifty years old—asked if she could take a stuffed animal from the playroom with her. She needed something to hold. I think of that moment often. The weight these women carry isn't just what they've fled or survived—it's what they must continue to endure, day after day, as they try to rebuild lives in a country that hasn't yet decided if it will welcome them.

As the clock struck twelve and the sky lit up, we sat in the soft glow of presence. Not solutions. Not resolutions. Just presence. The children had fallen asleep under blankets on the floor. The adults spoke softly in four different languages. We had no confetti, no champagne, no countdown. But there was something sacred in that space—an ember of joy that hadn't been extinguished.

There was courage in the room that night. Not the kind you read about in heroic tales, but the kind born of endurance. The kind that makes homemade pizza and folds laundry and asks for a stuffed animal because holding something soft is sometimes all you can do.

That night, I held them in the Light. And even now, I still do.

2020 wasn't a year we wished to forget. It was a year that cracked something open. From its rubble, this ministry of hospitality and accompaniment—Casa Alterna at Atlanta Friends Meeting—was born. Not out of strategy, but out of love. Not from a plan, but from a need.

And on the threshold of a new year, we stood together. Wounded, yes—but also grateful.

At the Threshold
How might you offer hospitality that helps carry the weight others endure daily as they try to rebuild their lives?

No Place to Go

Omar was an older man, recently released from immigration detention—one of more than seventy individuals unexpectedly freed from Stewart Detention Center in a single day. The relief was immediate and profound, but so was the weight of what came next: where would he go?

It was during the height of the COVID pandemic when I took him to the grocery store. I remember how nervous he was. This was his first time navigating the United States, a country he had never lived in before. He didn't even know how to correctly wear a mask—his nostrils were left uncovered. That small gesture, so unfamiliar to him, felt like a quiet emblem of the vast new world he had stepped into.

Part of Omar still wanted to go home—the place his heart knew, even if his feet could not follow. And yet, here he was, standing on the edge of a future filled with uncertainty but also possibility.

That day, we spent hours together making phone calls, searching for people who might offer a hand. We shared a simple outdoor meal, careful to keep a safe distance. The quiet between us held a weight that words couldn't carry. Later, we walked the aisles of the grocery store, gathering essentials for the journey ahead—though none of us could say exactly what that journey would look like.

I wanted, more than anything, to find someone—anyone—who could make room for Omar in their heart and home. Someone who could offer not just shelter but a shared space of belonging and care.

The next day, Omar would board a bus to a new state, stepping forward with courage and hope into the unknown. His immigration case still hung in the balance, a cloud of unanswered questions. And yet, in his heart, he carried a quiet wish to one day return home.

What stood out most in Omar was not the uncertainty or hardship—but his deep, genuine gratitude and joy in simply being free.

At the Threshold
When have you had no clear place to go—and who or what offered you shelter beyond walls?

When the Van Turns Back

We were told three men would soon be released from immigration detention. Our small circle of friends and allies prepared, ready to greet them with open arms and steady hearts. We understood the deep significance of that moment—a glimpse of freedom after so much confinement, uncertainty, and fear.

The plan was simple. I would meet one man at the bus station, while others went to the airport to welcome the two arriving by ICE van. But then the unexpected happened: a phone call. The ICE van wasn't coming. It was turning back. The men were being sent back to detention.

The wrong men had been released.

Pause with me for a moment. Imagine what those men must have felt: the crushing weight of hope quickly shattered, the anguish of being seen as "mistakes," the pain of another night in a cage, away from family and any sense of safety. We don't know their full stories, but we know enough—of journeys marked by desperation, crossing borders and dangers to escape violence and find refuge. Of long months or years behind bars, fighting for recognition of their humanity and rights. At least one had loved ones waiting here, hearts tethered to hope.

But in the eyes of the system, they were errors, easily sent back.

This experience is not an isolated failure but a symptom of a larger brokenness. When people are detained, they are stripped of dignity, treated not as human beings but as cargo to be moved, stored, forgotten. And when they are returned—sometimes broken—there is no reckoning.

Radical hospitality pushes back against that dehumanization. It is an act of solidarity that says, "You matter. You are seen. You are worthy." It invites us to recognize the divine spark in those whom systems of power seek to erase, even as we face the hard truth of our own entanglements with these systems.

Yet this is not a time for despair without hope. It is a time for embodied hope—hope that insists on action, on prayer, on faith. Hope that the voices of the voiceless will echo in the halls of power. Prayers that the privileged will be freed from their illusions of superiority and self-sufficiency. Faith that the mighty will one day turn around and stop swimming upstream against the ever-flowing stream of justice.

Until then, we will keep walking the edges, finding freedom in small acts of welcome, and holding fast to the day when no one will ever be "turned around" again.

At the Threshold
How might you recognize the humanity in those whom society tries to erase or discard?

Su Casa es Su Casa

This story is a testament to what faithful, loving hospitality looks like over time—how small acts of love and solidarity, quietly nurtured, can grow into lasting, generational gifts. Though this journey began long before our time at Atlanta Friends Meeting, it carries forward the same spirit: welcoming immigrants, fostering equity, and building community beyond the limits of traditional systems.

For nearly two decades, a small group of immigrant families and friends quietly explored ways to create affordable housing in LaGrange, Georgia — the town we called home for over twenty-five years. This year, their shared vision reached a milestone.

Between 2002 and 2009, four immigrant families joined a cooperative housing arrangement with us, building equity together in the homes they lived in. In 2015, they asked to purchase their homes outright. We shifted to a no-interest installment sale plan, allowing their years of care and investment to become a down payment. Just yesterday, all four families signed the deeds — becoming first-time homeowners.

Arturo and his late wife Norma were the first to step into this experiment in 2002. Their story is one of profound love and resilience. Norma faced end-stage renal disease, managing dialysis at home without insurance and with little hope for a transplant. From this hardship, a compassionate idea was born: to provide affordable, stable housing that could support Norma's fragile health, Arturo's care, and their two young children's future.

The moment Arturo signed the deed was bittersweet, a promise fulfilled in Norma's memory. He made the final payment alongside Carla, his new spouse and longtime friend, herself a widow. Together with Carla's youngest son, they now have a place to call their own. What began in mourning has turned to dancing.

Thanks to the collective faithfulness and commitment to fairness and equity, these families have built, on average, about 85% equity in their homes — a remarkable achievement in America, and especially rare among first-wave Latinx immigrant families. For context, the typical Latinx family holds just 14.6% of the wealth of the average white family, and for many immigrant-headed households, that number is even lower. These families are defying the odds, and in doing so, creating a foundation to pass forward.

But this is more than wealth. This model has nurtured family and neighborhood stability, and quietly supported children's academic success. On average, these families have lived in their homes for nearly thirteen years — nearly double the typical long-term renter's stay. Their homes have become a sanctuary they don't plan to leave.

Their houses represent future inheritance for their children, but the benefits are already blooming in the youngest generation. Every child raised in these homes has either graduated high school on time or is on track to do so. This year, we celebrate our first female graduate from the housing collective — raised by a devoted single mother of two, she will be the first in her family to attend college. Like those before her, she carries the hope of this home into new possibilities.

When housing is rooted in justice and community—not landlord profits, compounding interest, or unchecked capitalism—children, families, and neighborhoods flourish. This story is one of hope and home.

Su casa es su casa: your house is your home.

At the Threshold
How have you seen—or how might you imagine—small acts of hospitality and fairness turning a house into a home and building stronger communities for the future?

A Mother Holds On

"I sustain myself with the love of family."
- Maya Angelou

This Is Mother's Day.

Two of our most recent guests at Casa Alterna, mothers just released from immigration detention, reminded me of something deeply true: motherhood embodies grace and love, yet too often it is met with cruel and unjust systems.

The first mother we hosted is from Brazil, a country recently marked by one of the worst atrocities committed by police against civilians in its history. Because of how asylum-seeking works, she and her partner had no choice but to leave their children in the care of relatives, hoping that if asylum is granted in the United States, their family could someday be reunited. After journeying through many countries across the Americas, they never imagined that seeking safety would lead to prolonged detention and separation—her in Georgia, her partner in California.

When she was finally released from detention, her eyes told a story of fear, grief, and exhaustion—the pain of leaving her children behind, the hardships of migration, the heartbreak of forced separation, the inhumanity of detention, and now receiving hospitality from strangers. Who wouldn't be overwhelmed by such a whirlwind of emotions? Through small acts of love, many smiles, and a trusty translation app, we offered what little consolation we could during this brief pit stop on her path toward defiant hope.

The second mother we welcomed has lived in the United States for over twenty years. Her life here has been marked by struggle—low-wage jobs, the betrayal of a partner, the deportation of a son, and surviving sex trafficking. Yet, this single mother carries hope with fierce determination, pressing onward for a better life for herself and her U.S. citizen children, including one with special needs.

As soon as we learned she had been released, I reached out to one of her daughters, who speaks American English with a hint of Southern accent. The daughter was ecstatic and relieved that her mother had been freed from ICE's grip and that she could stay safely with us until the family could bring her home.

The next morning, after a seven-hour drive split between two vehicles packed with children, grandchildren, and family members, they arrived—each person eager to welcome the matriarch home. This mother is deeply loved, and her family wanted her to know it.

This is Mother's Day. Mothering is hard work, but it is also a gift of grace and love. May we celebrate those who mother us—and may we commit ourselves to dismantling the systems that treat mothers without grace, without love.

At the Threshold
How can we better support and stand alongside mothers who hold on through unimaginable hardship?

The Grit of Life

In one 24-hour cycle:

Eight strangers crossed our threshold—and became friends.

I led a virtual workshop on our practice of radical hospitality in a time of pandemic.

Then: bedtime.

At dawn, we rose to take our guests to the airport, each on the brink of reunion with loved ones. Not back home, but here, in the United States.

Then: a flat tire. 5:30 a.m.

So we walked in the drizzle to the train station, five jubilant companions and me. None had slept a wink, too elated by the promise of liberation. One man was preparing to see his mother for the first time in 38 years.

At the airport, we learned that one traveler's flight was indeed on the right date—just the wrong month. We fixed that.

Later, I introduced an asylum-seeking companion from West Africa to an iconic Southern institution: Waffle House. Over hot coffee and unfamiliar fare, I tried, unsuccessfully, to explain grits via a translation app. I was determined; she was not persuaded.

I returned home by public transportation and napped. While I slept, AAA came and replaced the tire.

That evening, Charlotte, Isaac—one of our long-term residents—and I gathered around the piano. He taught us hymns from his West African homeland. We taught him a few spirituals in return. As he picked up the melody, his powerful voice filled the Meeting Room:

"Were you there when he rose up from the tomb?"

I trembled.

Later that night, our door opened again. A new guest arrived: an 18-year-old asylum seeker, separated from her two younger siblings during their migration. No parent had accompanied them. She spent three months in ICE custody. Within 24 hours, she would be reunited with her siblings.

These are the rhythms of welcome.

These are the quiet mercies and fierce moments of joy that meet us in the grit of life.

At the Threshold
When life pulls you into unexpected detours and sacred interruptions, how might you stay rooted in the quiet mercies and fierce joys that come from welcoming others as kin?

Joy Took the Wheel

Hospitality is sometimes a joyride with wings.

On an ordinary summer day, we welcomed Valentin to Casa Alterna.

Valentin is an asylum seeker from South America, and this was his first full day of freedom in the United States. Having endured the long and uncertain journey that precedes seeking asylum in the United States, he now found himself with an abundance of something rare: free time. He wanted to explore. I was happy to oblige.

As we drove around, Valentin marveled at the lush, rolling hills of Atlanta. "So green," he kept saying, his eyes wide with wonder. "And so many trees!" To someone newly arrived from a border detention center, Atlanta's canopy of oaks and pines and the freedom of movement must have felt otherworldly.

Eventually, we turned our attention to a small task: picking up a donated futon for future guests. When we arrived at the donor's home, we quickly realized the futon was larger than my vehicle could reasonably accommodate.

But reason wasn't going to stop us.

We weren't far from the meetinghouse, just a mile, so I had an idea that surely raised a few eyebrows along the way. We hoisted the futon onto the roof of my car, its armrests sticking out like improvised wings.

Then I turned to Valentin with a grin and said, "In the United States, it's customary for an honored guest to ride atop the car like royalty. Would you like the seat of honor?"

He burst out laughing.

I added, "With these wings, if I drive fast enough, we might just take off and fly you straight to your new home up north."

More laughter.

It wasn't just about the futon, or even the ride. It was about joy. It was about crafting a moment of levity in a life that had been heavy. It was about welcoming a new friend with delight.

Thanks to our generous donor, we received more than just a piece of furniture. We received an opportunity to make Valentín's first day in America not only hospitable, but also unforgettable. Sometimes, hospitality looks like shelter. Other times, it looks like laughter shared over a futon strapped to a car and a flight of imagination on the streets of Atlanta.

At the Threshold
What might it look like for you to welcome someone not just with shelter or safety, but with joy that lets laughter and delight take the wheel?

Béni's Attitude

Jesus says the meek are blessed—the gentle, the humble, the nonviolent. The violent inherit nothing but blood and destruction. The meek, they inherit the earth.
— Father John Dear

Just before we loaded into the car that would take him to the airport and into the arms of his wife, Béni turned to me and spoke a blessing:

"God is going to bless your life and fill it with joy overflowing because God is a good God. This week, God will do the seemingly impossible for you and those you love."

His words stopped me.

In this work of hospitality, expressions of thanks are common. But this—this was something different. It wasn't just gratitude. It was benediction. And it came from a man who had every reason to be bitter.

Béni's story, like so many who find their way to our threshold, is woven with grief, faith, and astonishing resilience. He and his wife fled Haiti several years ago, their homeland crumbling under the weight of violence, natural disaster, and a government that could no longer guarantee life or liberty. Together, they crossed waters and borders, holding tight to each other and the dream of a future where they could live in dignity.

By the time they reached the U.S. border, Béni's wife was pregnant. What followed is all too familiar: they asked for asylum and were met not with welcome, but with handcuffs. They were separated and locked up in different detention centers—warehouses for the unwanted, places that grind people down and call it due process.

And then the unthinkable: Béni's wife suffered a miscarriage while in custody.

He shared this devastating loss with a quiet honesty, never once assigning blame. Not to his wife. Not to God. Not even to the cruel machinery of immigration enforcement that had separated them and withheld care. Of course he mourned. How could he not? But he bore his grief with a kind of grace I don't fully understand.

I didn't tell him how angry I felt. Angry that our nation—a nation I love—allowed this to happen. Angry that women in detention are routinely denied even the most basic care. Angry that the very system that promised "the legal way" to seek asylum became a gauntlet of suffering.

And yet, it was Béni who laid his hand on my shoulder and spoke a word of hope over my life.

He didn't offer that blessing because I had earned it.

He offered it because he knows who he is—a beloved child of God. His faith isn't a posture or a performance. It's the marrow of his bones. He has seen death, and still he speaks life.

In that sacred moment, I found myself standing on holy ground—not because of anything I had done, but because Béni, the one supposedly in need of sanctuary, became a sanctuary to me.

This is the strange and beautiful paradox of hospitality: when we open our doors to welcome others, we find ourselves being welcomed too—welcomed into lives marked by courage, grief, faith, and fierce love.

Béni's life reminds me of the beatitudes—the blessings Jesus spoke over those the world tends to ignore or cast aside. His presence among us is a living testimony to that upside-down kingdom where the last are first and the meek inherit the earth.

Blessed is Béni, for his is the kingdom of heaven.

Blessed is Béni, who comforts others even as he mourns.

Blessed is Béni, whose meekness has carried him across many lands.

Blessed is Béni, whose hunger and thirst for righteousness fill the heart.

Blessed is Béni, whose words of mercy reveal his trust in a merciful God.

Blessed is Béni, for in the purity of his heart, he sees God.

Béni's attitude wasn't one of anger, despair, or self-pity—though all would have been justified. His was the posture of someone who knows, deep in his bones, that God is still good. That hope is still possible. That joy can still overflow. His attitude reflected the same blessing-filled vision Jesus spoke on that hillside so long ago: a kingdom where the grieving are comforted, the meek inherit the earth, and mercy multiplies.

Béni's attitude is a beatitude.

A way of seeing. A way of trusting. A way of blessing others—even from the wilderness.

At the Threshold
How might your heart and hospitality be transformed if you saw the meek—not as powerless—but as bearers of blessing, joy, and unshakable hope even in the midst of loss?

Surely, God is With Us

At Casa Alterna, we recently reached a milestone: our 400th guest arrived. To mark this moment, Katie, a new volunteer, and I took Jorge and Yeldín—our guests #400 and #401—to a small local restaurant serving food from their homeland. There is something heartwarming about sharing a meal that reminds you of home. Hospitality often begins at the table, where food becomes more than nourishment—it becomes a language of welcome, a bridge across cultures, a place where strangers become friends.

Welcoming someone new is more than opening a door. It is an invitation to step into the unknown with an open heart, embracing the unfamiliar as though they were a long-lost friend. Hospitality is an act of mutual recognition, honoring that of God within each of us. Around that table, Jorge and Yeldín were not simply guests; they became hosts, sharing memories and stories through the flavors of their country. As Ed Loring, co-founder of the Open Door

Community, often said: justice is important, but supper is essential.

There is a rhythm to hospitality, a sacred ebb and flow of giving and receiving. When we offer shelter, a meal, or a kind word, we do so knowing we also receive. We receive the stories, the laughter, the songs, and even the silences that speak louder than words. Hospitality is not a one-way street but a circle of presence and welcome, where the boundaries between host and guest blur and the divine is found in the encounter itself.

Why mention the $400 cash we had? If you know me, you know this was not about splurging. The meal was modest, made even more affordable by the generosity of the restaurant owner, herself an immigrant who takes pride in welcoming fellow travelers with un sabor de su tierra—a taste of home. She understands, as we do, that these small acts carry enormous weight, that a meal shared in kindness can be a balm for weary souls.

After paying, I divided the remaining cash equally between Jorge and Yeldín and offered a blessing for their journey ahead. Jorge's eyes filled with tears as he turned to Yeldín and said, "Seguramente, Dios está con nosotros." Surely, God is with us.

This simple phrase carries a profound truth that shapes the work we do and the lives we touch. It is the deep truth we live by—that God is always with us. Not a distant deity far removed from human suffering or joy, but a presence that draws near, shows up in real time, around real tables, among real people seeking refuge and belonging.

God was not in the cash, but surely in the hearts of

those who give, and in the spirit of those who receive. Just as God dwelled within Mary, the migrant mother who bore the world's hope despite having no room, so God dwells within every one of us who welcomes and is welcomed.

Each guest who crosses our threshold carries their own story—a story often marked by hardship, loss, and courage. Yet in their presence, we glimpse the enduring strength of the human spirit, the seeds of hope planted in soil too often scorched by injustice. To welcome is to witness that resilience, to honor it, and to walk alongside it.

In a world too often divided by fear and suspicion, hospitality is a radical act of trust and faith. It is a quiet rebellion against the walls that separate us, a living testimony to the belief that love is stronger than fear. To offer shelter, to share a meal, to listen deeply—these are the ways we say, without words, "You belong here."

Yes, God is with us. And more than that, God is within us.

At the Threshold

How might opening your heart and table to others reveal the presence of the divine within them—and transform your understanding of hospitality as a shared act of hope and trust?

2022 - 2024
Where the Journey Meets Welcome

Every journey holds the power to both break and remake us. For many asylum seekers and vulnerable immigrants, the path is long—fraught with danger, separation, and profound uncertainty. Yet it is also a journey toward freedom, hope, and unexpected grace. Over these years, as a tsunami of asylum seekers—primarily from Venezuela—arrived, Casa Alterna responded with a deepening commitment to be a place where such journeys meet welcome.

What began as simple acts of hospitality grew into a transitional housing program that offered more than shelter: a space for healing and rebuilding. Casa Alterna expanded its reach, including spinning off its airport accompaniment ministry that met newcomers at their first point of arrival.

In walking alongside these travelers, I encountered remarkable people whose stories revealed not only the harsh realities of fleeing violence and injustice, but also the deep reservoirs of faith and love that sustain them.

Their footsteps mapped a path not only across geography, but through courage, sacrifice, and unwavering trust in something greater than themselves.

As their lives intersected with the hospitality of strangers, we witnessed how even the most daunting journeys could become pathways to healing and belonging. This is a time of transformation—for them and for us—where the journey and the welcome meet, shaping each other in unexpected and gracious ways.

One Long Journey

Life is one long journey. Along the way, we face unexpected turns—moments when we long to turn back, but cannot. The road is often harsh, full of barriers that seem insurmountable. Yet, it is also a path where freedom takes root, hope endures, and love leads the way.

Recently, four women arrived—each carrying a story of a long, difficult journey.

Victoria came to us, separated by ICE from her father and her thirteen-year-old brother. Barely an adult herself, she endured the loneliness and cruelty of detention. But even behind cold walls and iron bars, something unshakable remained: a faith that sets the spirit free. When the guards called "count" over and over, Victoria and the women around her turned those moments into prayers—quiet acts of resistance and hope. In a place designed to break spirits, faith became her lifeline, a steady flame of hope. For Victoria, life is a long journey sustained by freedom born in faith.

Then there is Dolores, who made the wrenching decision to leave her children behind, hoping to build a better future for them. Her journey north was brutal—hours spent cramped inside the trailer of a tractor-trailer, alongside dozens of others. She learned to sleep standing up, breathing shallow in the suffocating air, fearing the darkness and the unknown. Fasting was not just spiritual but practical, a way to avoid using a filthy, exposed toilet. Days passed in a blur, the world outside invisible. And still, hope was her anchor—the hope that one day, her children would live without fear or want. For Dolores, life is a long journey carried on the wings of hope.

And then, two Anas—a mother and daughter—sharing not only a name but an unbreakable bond. With just thirteen dollars between them and a single phone's GPS, they traveled more than two thousand miles. Against the odds, they trusted in a God who never abandons. In a world quick to judge and slow to care, they chose to believe in the kindness of strangers, walking forward by faith alone. Like Ruth and Naomi before them, they vowed:

"Where you go, I will go; where you lodge, I will lodge; your people shall be my people, and your God my God. Where you die, I will die—there will I be buried."

For these two Anas, life is a long journey defined by a love that never walks alone.

Yes, life is one long journey. The forks in the road may bring uncertainty, but they also invite freedom. Every heartbreaking setback can become a messenger of hope. And every time we carry one another's burdens, we remember this truth: the topography and destination of our journey is one and the same—love.

At the Threshold
How might your heart open to see those traveling this long road not as strangers, but as fellow pilgrims whose courage invites you to walk alongside them?

The Gift of a Mirror

"Rather than basing immigration reform on the virtue of hospitality, I would suggest that [the church] further wrestle with the Christian responsibility of restitution."
— Rev. Dr. Miguel A. de la Torre

I carry a hypothesis that's both painful and true: the more "Black Lives Matter" signs that bloom in a neighborhood, the more likely it is that Black neighbors have been pushed out by gentrification's erasure. When we're feeling a little sharper with words, we might imagine a companion sign that reads, "Gentrification: Black Lives Scatter." It's a mirror we don't always want to hold up, but one that demands our attention.

Hospitality is a spiritual practice. It is a lens that reveals what our hearts truly believe—not just about others, but about ourselves. The challenge is that we often wear blinders shaped by culture and privilege, blinders that prevent us from seeing ourselves clearly, and blinders that keep us from recognizing the sacredness in those who walk through our doors.

Many who claim the name of Jesus still fail to see our own racism. We cannot recognize Christ in those we dismiss or fear. And many who carry the banner of justice and equity live in silos of privilege—segregated by education, race, or class—never fully encountering the lives we profess to stand with. Even with the best intentions, these blind spots keep us from hospitality rooted in genuine solidarity and mutual transformation.

Welcoming vulnerable immigrants has become a sacred mirror for me. It has reflected back not only the hardness of my assumptions but the depth of my privilege as a First World citizen. It demands that we listen—truly listen—beyond our own stories and biases. It calls us to affirm the courage and dignity of Black and Brown migrants who—as Miguel de la Torre insists—are not merely recipients of our welcome but rightful claimants of justice and restitution.

Hospitality also reveals what we believe about God.

I remember breaking bread with Joaquín, a guest who had fled unimaginable pain. We sat in a small restaurant serving food from his homeland. Over familiar flavors, Joaquín shared the grief of his father's recent murder—the very reason he had fled. Unable to bring his children with him, his young adult daughter now cares for her teenage brother alone, in a home he left behind with both love and fear.

His grief mingled with gratitude and guilt. Joaquín

spoke with the faith of a psalmist, certain God had guided him through every danger: "A thousand may fall at your side, ten thousand at your right hand, but it will not come near you." Yet the sorrow of separation from his children hung heavy between us. He spoke quietly of debts to repay, of money he must send to keep his family safe.

In that moment, all we could offer was our presence—wholehearted and undistracted. I held him in the Light and prayed with a steady heart: "Joaquín, God holds you, your children, your hopes, and your fears. You are God's beloved."

Hospitality is indeed the gift of a mirror. It reflects our assumptions and longings, our limitations and faith. And if we dare to look deeply, it has the power to transform how we see others—and how we see ourselves.

At the Threshold
How might your hospitality become a mirror revealing hidden assumptions and privileges—and propel you toward the harder work of restitution and solidarity with those you welcome?

On Prophets and "Pastorcitos"

Everyone is welcome.

That's the message posted at the entrance of the Atlanta Friends Meetinghouse, where we live, worship, and extend hospitality through Casa Alterna. It's more than a sentiment. It's a spiritual commitment.

In a world where many have grown weary of both church and state—where political dogma often replaces spiritual depth, and institutional loyalty eclipses the work of love—we find ourselves drawn toward something both ancient and urgently needed. We long to embody a sacred alternative: a way of being rooted in Spirit, shaped by justice, and animated by welcome.

Since opening the doors of the meetinghouse as a place of refuge for asylum seekers, hundreds of guests from across the globe have passed through—each one carrying not just stories of hardship, but gifts of resilience, courage, and sacred presence. These are not mere numbers. These are names. Faces. Lives bearing the image of God.

Among them is a boy named Israel.

Israel arrived in the United States with his young parents after an unfathomable journey—through the jungle of the Darién Gap, across Central America and Mexico, and finally to what they hoped would be a place of safety. But instead of sanctuary, they found themselves stranded in a borderland shelter with no clear path forward.

Then came a whisper of hope. A fellow traveler said, "Go to Atlanta. Churches there will help." With nothing more than that fragile promise, they boarded a bus to a city they did not know. Guided not by a GPS but by what they describe as an angel—disguised as a man on the street—they found their way to City Hall. From there, we got the call. And we opened the door.

When we met, Israel began calling me "Pastor." I told him "Anton" was just fine. But he insisted. So I responded in kind, calling him Pastorcito—little pastor. These days, he prefers I call him "Israel," but with the English pronunciation. I don't mind. I smile every time he says my name.

If I am, in his eyes, a pastoral presence, I hope he knows this: I see that of God in him.

This isn't poetic metaphor—it's a spiritual conviction. A foundational truth in the Quaker tradition and in the Gospel: that there is that of God in everyone. To believe this is to insist that no one is disposable. No one is illegal. No one arrives at our door without sacred worth.

This belief demands more than sentiment. It demands action. It calls us to open the doors of our sanctuaries not only to worshippers but to the weary. To share not just prayers but shelter. To recognize that hospitality is not a service project—it is a spiritual practice. A form of resistance. A daily defiance of a world that criminalizes migration, cages children, and elevates borders over belonging.

Dorothy Day once called our dominant systems a "filthy, rotten system." She wasn't wrong. But the invitation of Christ is to something else entirely—a beloved community where we "welcome one another as Christ has welcomed us," not as strangers or servants, but as friends.

In Israel, I glimpse that friendship. I see a shepherd's heart forming in a boy's frame. I see joy that has survived treacherous miles. I see God's image—unmistakable, unearned, and unerasable.

If the children shall lead us, then I am glad to follow Pastorcito for a while.

At the Threshold

Who are the "pastorcitos" in your life—the unexpected prophets whose presence, questions, or naming of you invite you to live more fully into love, justice, and welcome?

Crisis or Community?

"One of the great liabilities of history is that all too many people fail to remain awake through great periods of social change. Today, our very survival depends on our ability to stay awake, to adjust to new ideas, to remain vigilant and to face the challenge of change."
— Martin Luther King Jr., Where Do We Go From Here: Chaos or Community?

Since 2014, millions of Venezuelans have fled their homeland—parents, children, elders walking away from repression, economic collapse, and hunger. Nearly three-quarters of the country now lives on less than two dollars a day. But statistics never tell the whole story. What carries people through jungle and desert, over bridges and borders, is something deeper: a desperate hope for dignity.

Over the past two years, we at Casa Alterna have received dozens of Venezuelan asylum seekers. Most stayed just a night or two—long enough to catch their breath before reuniting with family in Miami, New York, or beyond. But this summer brought a shift. Venezuelans began arriving in Atlanta not because someone was waiting for them, but because no one was. No one to receive them. No address to give Immigration and Customs Enforcement (ICE). No place to call home.

In a matter of months, ten individuals found themselves in need of long-term shelter. And they are not alone. In the past two weeks alone, we've had to turn away more than a dozen others.

Why Atlanta? Word spreads quickly through migrant social media. Atlanta is rumored to be a city of opportunity—with jobs, affordable rent, even promises of a year's housing or a $600 food voucher. None of this is true. But hope, especially in desperation, clings to whatever possibility it can find.

ICE requires asylum seekers processed in Texas to provide a U.S. address—something stable in the midst of instability. When someone says "Atlanta" but has nowhere to go, ICE agents have occasionally listed old, unconfirmed, or entirely fictitious addresses. People arrive confused and disoriented, dropped into a city they do not know, carrying paperwork tied to a place that does not exist.

Most come from the Migrant Resource Center in San Antonio, a 450-bed shelter overwhelmed by the volume of need. The staff—Catholic Charities, city workers, volunteers—do their best to offer support and one-way bus tickets. But verifying every destination in such a high-traffic environment is nearly impossible.

What's unfolding here is a quiet crisis. Not declared, not broadcast, but real. The new arrivals come with nothing but names, court dates, and a fragile sense of trust in the rumor of welcome.

And Atlanta is not ready. Not yet.

But readiness has never been the precondition for compassion.

Casa Alterna recently opened a second hospitality house in partnership with Atlanta Mennonite Church. Faithful families have opened spare rooms. Other groups are stepping up with food, hotel vouchers, and informal support. Soon, for the first time, we will gather the patchwork of service providers to begin imagining a shared response.

Still, there is no illusion of scale. The need far exceeds the capacity. And yet we persist. Hospitality is not about solving every problem. It's about showing up anyway—with soup, with shelter, with solidarity.

Dr. King's dream of the Beloved Community was never abstract. It was embodied in meals shared, doors opened, burdens carried. He knew that what stood in the way of justice wasn't always hate. Sometimes it was indifference. Or delay. Or red tape.

So here we are again, in the valley of decision.

The arrival of these asylum seekers is not just a policy matter. It is a moral moment. A spiritual invitation.

Will we respond with bureaucracy, or with belonging?

Crisis or community?

The choice is ours.

At the Threshold
When a stranger arrives with nothing but hope and a name, how does your body respond—and what might it be telling you about the kind of community you're being called to help create?

They Carry Hope

We recently welcomed Dolores, an unhoused asylum seeker from the Caribbean. Medically fragile and facing a complicated diagnosis, Dolores had made the anguishing decision to leave her teenage son behind in the care of her sister. She came alone, hoping that in this country, her body might stand a better chance of healing.

Along the way, she fell in with two fellow travelers—men who, like her, had left behind their homes in search of safety. They made a kind of kinship on the road, each one bolstered by the other's presence. They agreed to journey together to Atlanta, where they hoped opportunity might greet them.

But the unspoken hierarchies of gender and power made quick work of their solidarity. Upon arrival, the three were separated. Shelters sorted them into categories. Dolores—without a working phone—was left alone in a city that had never promised to catch her. The men disappeared into their own struggles. The tenuous threads she had clung to dissolved. She ended up in a shelter, grateful for a bed but living under the clock. Thirty days. Then, no more.

That's when she came to stay with us.

For a few days, our home became her threshold. Off the streets, away from institutional time limits, she rested. We shared meals. We told stories. We prayed in silence. We waited. We did not offer healing. We simply offered presence.

And in that presence, something holy took root.

In the simple act of giving and receiving shelter, the room filled with grace. It wasn't loud or dramatic. It came in the quiet, in the gentle clinking of forks on plates, in the shared understanding that this, too, was church. Not a building. A body. A table. A tired soul finding room to breathe.

Thanks to the care of others in our wider community, Dolores now has temporary housing in a rural corner of Georgia. I don't know what the next chapter holds for her. I'm not sure if she'll ever live independently again. But for now, she is safe. And that is no small thing. That is sacred ground.

Soon, Fernando will return.

Fernando first came to us not long ago. He had just arrived in the U.S., fleeing violence in a South American homeland with his cousin. Released from detention, but separated from the only family member he had left, Fernando needed somewhere to wait—somewhere to remember that he wasn't alone.

He stayed with us for a few nights—quiet, attentive,

unsure of what came next. After his cousin was released, we stayed in touch. Almost daily. But their bond was soon tested. Hidden addictions surfaced. The fragile hope they carried fractured under the pressure.

So now, Fernando is returning. Not just to a familiar bed and meal, but to a circle of care. A home that remembers him. A space that honors both his grief and his grit. He is not a problem to be solved. He is a life to be held.

This season holds so much: injustice and gratitude, grief and generosity, weariness and wonder. But above all, it holds Dolores and Fernando—beloved travelers whose courage to keep moving toward hope reminds us why we keep our doors open.

Because every time we do, something sacred walks in with them.

At the Threshold
What might change in you if you received others not as burdens to bear, but as bearers of a grace you didn't know you needed?

Beloved and Cradled

"Here is the world. Beautiful and terrible things will happen. Don't be afraid. I am with you. Nothing can ever separate us. It's for you I created the universe. I love you."
— Frederick Buechner

Oscar and I sat down for breakfast at a modest diner in Atlanta. Oscar's first bite of crispy, golden hash browns brought a faint smile to his face. In that simple moment, amid a journey marked by violence and loss, grace found its way.

More than food, this breakfast became a sacred space—a quiet altar where stories could be carried without fear. Oscar carried the weight of horrors too raw to speak aloud. He was no exception to the common thread of suffering that binds many who flee.

Oscar is a truck driver from South America. One day on the road, masked guerrillas ambushed him and other drivers, seizing trucks and setting some ablaze. The violence rippled beyond his country's borders, leaving wounds that would not easily heal.

At the same time, his wife Myrna was pregnant with their first child. Faced with imminent birth and escalating danger, they made the painful choice to leave behind home and community in search of safety. But when a clerical error denied Myrna a passport, the family was forced to make an impossible decision.

Myrna could not risk the perilous migrant routes with the baby coming so soon. Oscar, meanwhile, could no longer wait in a place overshadowed by fear. So he set out alone, seeking asylum, while Myrna stayed behind to welcome their newborn son, Oscar Jr., into a world still crying out for justice and peace.

As the waitress poured Oscar another cup of coffee, he pulled out his phone.

"I want to show you something," he said.

"This is the last photo I took with my son on my last day with him. He was only two weeks old."

The image was more than a memory—it was a quiet testament to fierce love and deep loss. Oscar cradled his son with a gentleness that defied the cruelty surrounding them.

I held the phone with care, searching for words to honor his pain without offering empty consolation.

"It is so clear how deeply you love your son. I see it—in the way you hold him, in your eyes, and in the brave story you've shared. No loving parent chooses separation. No parent wants to leave their child in a world so often unkind and unsafe."

A tear traced down Oscar's cheek.

Then I said softly, "There is another sacred image here, too. What if, in this moment, God is the loving parent and you are the beloved child cradled in God's arms? The uncertainty remains, but how might seeing this photo through that lens change its meaning?"

Oscar looked again at the photo. His breath steadied in a sacred pause.

"I am not alone," he whispered.

At the Threshold

Imagine you are holding Oscar's photo in your hand, how might embracing the truth that you, too, are deeply beloved and cradled in love transform the way you face your own moments of loss and uncertainty?

The Welcome Table

Bonita held her infant granddaughter close as she stepped off the bus into the heavy Georgia air. The sun hung low, casting long shadows over the city and her hopes. She had come with her adult daughter, driven by a longing that defied reason—a fierce and unrelenting love determined to make it to rural southwest Georgia where the daughter's husband was detained by immigration authorities—determined to keep the family whole in a land that often renders people invisible.

They had no lawyer. No plan. No money to offer. Only love.

Their first stop was the Atlanta ICE field office, seeking mercy that was not given. What Bonita and her family heard loud and clear in the indifference was: You do not belong here.

Ten years in this country had not earned them a seat at the table. Their grief went unseen. Their hope was disregarded.

But love, stubborn as it is, does not vanish when ignored. It looks for a way in.

Sometimes that way is a table.

I brought Bonita and her family to a restaurant serving food from her homeland to meet three seminarians from Candler School of Theology. These students did not come to fix or preach but arrived with open ears, hungry hearts, and tentative Spanish. Around that table, carried gently by my translation and by shared meals, something sobering yet sacred unfolded.

No immigration status changed. No system shifted.

But something in Bonita's eyes softened, and that moment held its own kind of grace.

She said quietly, "This is the first time I have ever been made to feel welcome by an American in this country." The first time.

There are powers in the world that build walls and seal borders. But there is another power—one that builds tables in the wilderness and says, Welcome, Friends.

It does not make headlines. It is not fluent in law or powerful in court.

But it knows how to listen. It knows how to break bread. And it knows that sometimes liberation arrives quietly in the sharing of a meal among strangers who recognize something holy that had been disguised.

This is not a story of rescue or revolution. It is a story of prophetic presence.

We did not change Bonita's uncertain future. But we changed her present experience by seeing the image of

God within her.

Perhaps that is where the deeper work begins—in being welcomed before being documented, in being befriended before being vetted by a fear-laden system.

Radical hospitality is not soft or easy. It is the hard, patient labor of transforming the world one shared table, one human connection at a time.

Bonita's words still echo—a lament and an invitation:

"This is the first time I have ever been made to feel welcome by an American in this country."

May it never be the last time she is welcomed at the table.

At the Threshold
How might you create a welcome table in your own life—one where those who feel unseen and unheard can be met with presence, dignity, and belonging?

The Quinceañera and the One-Armed Companion

A story of love that embraces brokenness, teaching us how compassion grows in the spaces where wounds remain.

The day was radiant, full of warmth and hope, as scores of family and friends gathered in Guatemala City to celebrate Britany's quinceañera. She is the beloved sister of our godson Manny, and over the years, our bond has deepened—woven through visits, stories, and shared tenderness. Britany's life has not been easy, shaped by hardship but also by a deep, unwavering love that carries her like sacred threads.

As I stood among family and friends, invited to offer a reflection, a memory came forward—one that speaks to the quiet power of connection and the kind of love that crosses borders and brokenness alike.

In the early days of Manny's life, tragic circumstances led to his mother's imprisonment and subsequent deportation. In that tender time, my wife Charlotte and I stepped forward, becoming his guardians for his first fifteen months.

During those nights, infant Manny found comfort in a well-worn stuffed rabbit named Bo. More than a toy, Bo was a companion and refuge. Even now, at eleven, Manny still sleeps soundly with his faithful plush friend.

Over time, Bo grew worn and weary—one of his arms came off. But Manny's love remained steadfast. Bo's imperfection only deepened their bond.

When Britany was twelve, she chose to create a new companion for Bo. She named it Boa—and with deliberate care, she made Boa with just one arm, mirroring Bo's own imperfection.

She did not try to fix Bo's story. She honored it.

In that simple act, Britany showed a wisdom beyond her years. True compassion does not erase wounds—it journeys alongside them. Her gesture was quietly prophetic, making visible what our world often hides or rushes past: brokenness does not disqualify us from love. Rather, it is the soil where love can take its deepest root.

That day, we were not only celebrating a quinceañera. We were witnessing the radical empathy Britany embodies—a love that embraces fragility, creates space for healing, and invites us to walk with one another through joy and struggle.

I am grateful that Bo has Boa. But more than that, I am grateful Manny and Britany have each other—companions bound by something far deeper than circumstance. Their love, forged in hardship and nurtured by community, is a living testament to hope.

May we all learn to love like that—with the tenderness of a one-armed companion and the faithful courage of a quinceañera.

At the Threshold
How might your heart open to loving and accompanying others—not by trying to fix their brokenness, but by honoring the sacred stories that their wounds carry?

The Border-Crossing Power of Love

"Be patterns, be examples in all countries, places, islands, nations, wherever you come."
—George Fox

At Casa Alterna, we have come to trust in the border-crossing power of love. What began with the humble act of offering shelter has grown into something deeper: an ever-evolving experiment in beloved community. Not a program. Not a mission. A way of life that transgresses fear, defies systems, and dares to believe that love, when embodied, can create the world we long for.

We never set out to build an organization. We said yes to a few people in need, and the yeses kept coming. What we've learned is that sacred resistance doesn't always look like protest—it often looks like presence. A clean bed. A shared table. A name spoken with tenderness. The revolutionary act of saying: You belong here.

Two Doorways into Welcome

Today, our hospitality unfolds in two different yet intertwined spaces.

At the Atlanta Friends Meetinghouse, we receive asylum seekers for short stays—often just a night or two. They come from detention, from the border, from journeys no one should ever have to endure. They arrive carrying stories that strain the heart—stories of extortion, loss, terror, and survival. But what meets them here is not bureaucracy or suspicion. It is warmth. A home-cooked meal. A porch light left on. Someone to ask, "How was your journey?" and wait long enough to listen.

Just across the city, a house has become a second threshold—a space for long-term transitional living. Those who enter this home are not clients. They are neighbors. Women from Cuba, young adults from Venezuela, survivors from Guatemala and Honduras. They share life with residential allies: people who have chosen to live in community, side by side, with those in exile. This is not charity. It is kinship. We do not fix each other—we make space for each other to heal.

And somehow, against the grain of the world, this works. Meals are shared. Children are tucked in. Gardens are tended. Conflicts arise and are resolved. It is messy and beautiful, exhausting and life-giving. And it is holy ground.

The Jungle We Don't See

The more I listen to our guests, the more I see the American asylum system for what it is: a second jungle.

Many who have arrived at our doorsteps have already crossed the Darién Gap—that lawless, deadly stretch of jungle between Colombia and Panama. It is a place of unspeakable suffering. But the suffering doesn't stop when they reach the U.S. border. It only changes form.

Here, the terrain is not physical but bureaucratic—and no less treacherous. People who have already risked their lives are forced into legal limbo. After passing their "credible fear" interviews, which affirm that their claim might be valid, they are still left with no way to work, no public defender, no access to housing or food assistance.

The system demands urgency while withholding the means to respond. Most asylum seekers have only one year to file their claim. But how do you gather documentation, navigate a foreign legal system, and find a trustworthy attorney—without money, without language, without rest?

And even when they submit their application, they must wait six more months before they're eligible to request a work permit. It's a cruel paradox: you must act quickly, but you cannot support yourself while doing so.

This isn't about law and order. It's about power and exclusion. And in immigration court, even geography becomes destiny. In Atlanta, only 13% of asylum claims are approved. In New York, it's closer to 70%. That gap doesn't reflect the strength of the claims. It reflects the mood of the bench. The whims of politics. The randomness of borders.

Love as Sacred Resistance

In the face of all this, we do not retreat. We lean in. Hospitality, when rooted in love and sustained by community, becomes a form of sacred resistance. It is not a handout—it is a defiant affirmation of human worth.

Each meal shared around the table pushes back against the story that some lives are disposable. Each night of shelter offered is a small refusal to comply with cruelty. Each moment of companionship becomes a sermon without words: You are not alone. You are not forgotten. You are not a case file. You are kin.

This kind of hospitality is not always efficient. It is rarely easy. But it is powerful, because it is personal. It unravels the fear that systems rely on. It builds trust where trauma once lived. And it teaches us that accompaniment is not a one-way act—it transforms the one who welcomes as much as the one who arrives.

Becoming the Pattern

There's no blueprint for what we're doing. We are simply trying to live in the pattern of love.

George Fox's invitation—to be examples wherever we go—rings in my ears often. Not because we are perfect, but because we are willing. Willing to be present in the mess. Willing to listen longer than is comfortable. Willing to open our homes, even when the world tells us to close our doors.

Over time, these small, faithful acts have stitched something beautiful together. They have formed a community not of saviors, but of sojourners. People on the road, walking each other home.

We do not always know what to do. But we try to live as if the Kingdom is already among us. We prepare a

room. We set the table. We make the coffee strong.
>And we keep saying yes.
>Not because it fixes everything.
>Because love doesn't stop at the border.
>Love begins there.

At the Threshold
How might your life change if you chose to welcome others not as a duty, but as a faithful act—believing that in preparing a place for them, you might also discover your own place in the story of love, justice, and belonging?

A Sanctuary of Love

"Mercy triumphs over judgment."
—James 2:13

I didn't go looking for Glenda and her baby. I was visiting a nearby organization, exploring ways we might deepen our collective response to the needs of asylum seekers. I came expecting a conversation about systems and strategy. But instead, I met Daniel—nine months old, soft-eyed and wide-smiled, crawling into my heart.

His mother, Glenda, was young and soft-spoken, but carried herself with a quiet strength. There was nothing dramatic in the way she spoke of their situation. No self-pity. Just facts. She and her son had nowhere safe to stay. No bed. No crib. No family nearby. The threat of homelessness wasn't looming—it was already here.

Sometimes, discernment doesn't wait for deliberation. I invited them to stay at our Quaker meetinghouse—a sanctuary where hospitality is a way of life, not just a gesture. She said yes.

Their time with us was brief—just a few days—but it mattered. A pause. A breath. A place to be seen, to rest safely, to imagine next steps without the immediate fear of where to go next.

We were already full, but welcome isn't measured by bed counts. It's measured by whether someone feels they matter.

Kaitlyn, one of our resident allies, gave her day off to accompany Glenda and Daniel to the consulate, seeking answers. Then she treated them to a simple joy: lunch and a visit to the local aquarium. For Glenda, who had spent much of the past year confined to a small room in Atlanta, this day felt expansive. It was a reminder that life can still hold delight—that strangers can still surprise us with tenderness.

Eventually, Glenda made the decision to return to her home country. Not out of defeat, nor blind hope, but from a longing to be in her mother's arms, to place Daniel in family care, to try again in a place that, for all its dangers, also held pieces of her heart. We helped secure a flight and planned to accompany her to the airport.

I don't romanticize this part of the story. The broken systems that forced her here remain unchanged. Her return does not resolve the injustice. But what she received—and what she gave—is something those systems cannot touch: a glimpse of beloved community, however brief. A few days of rest. A few nights of peace. A sanctuary of love.

At the Threshold
What would it mean for you to make room—truly make room—for someone whose story is still unfolding, even when your own space feels full?

Beloved Strength: Welcoming New Life and Resilience

"It is a beautiful thing when folks in poverty are no longer just a missions project but become genuine friends and family with whom we laugh, cry, dream and struggle."
— Shane Claiborne

Casa Alterna is a home alive with beloved strength, where hope and resilience shape every breath. Recently, we welcomed two newborns into our shared life—Elián and Maria—whose arrival has deepened our sense of wonder and responsibility. Their gentle presence—soft breaths, coos, and delicate rhythms—reminds us that new life is always a call to deeper hospitality.

In these walls, stories converge: families who have traveled difficult paths, carrying both sorrow and courage. Now, with eleven residents here, including six children, our days hum with renewed energy. Yet the focus is not on numbers, but on the deeper commitment to nurture each life:

to hold infants tenderly, to listen to parents with empathy, and to weave a network of care that honors each person's dignity.

When you consider the meaning behind the names "Elián" and "Maria"—"beloved strength"—notice how they mirror the spirit animating this place. Each new life embodies hope's quiet power, inviting us to trust that love can transcend fear and uncertainty. In welcoming them, we acknowledge our own vulnerability: caring for newborns requires patience, attention, and a willingness to be changed by their needs. Yet precisely through this vulnerability, resilience grows—rooted in community, shared responsibility, and the conviction that no one among us stands alone.

As you observe the rhythms in your own context—whether through rituals, prayers, or moments of stillness—hold in your heart all who seek refuge and belonging. Reflect on how welcoming a stranger, or tending to a fragile life, transforms not only the newcomer but the entire household. In this mutual exchange, we discover that hospitality is not a one-way transaction but a dynamic process: we give welcome, and we are welcomed; we offer care, and we receive gifts of trust and connection.

This chapter invites you to see hospitality as a sacred practice: more than providing a roof or a meal, it is about creating space where dignity is affirmed and relationships flourish. In the quiet midnight feedings or the soft lullabies, we glimpse a profound truth: love is enacted in small, consistent acts that accumulate into something enduring. Resilience is born in shared nights of wakefulness, in collective laughter when a child's first smile appears, and in solidarity when challenges arise.

At Casa Alterna, every day brings both unpredictability and grace. Newborn life reminds us that hope is never abstract—it is embodied in the rhythms of feeding, in the embrace of a parent who has traversed hardship, and in the communal vigil of those who stand alongside. These moments teach us to trust in an unfolding future that we cannot control but can help shape through loving presence.

Consider how this resonates beyond our walls: in your circles, how might you extend this ethos of welcome? What practices nurture resilience when you encounter fragility—whether in a neighbor, a friend, or even within yourself? The arrival of Elián and Maria urges us to remember that every life, however small, carries the promise of transformation: for them, for us, and for the wider world.

Gratitude arises naturally—not as formal announcement but as an inner posture. We carry thankfulness for trust given by families, for the ways we learn from one another, and for the deepening of our own capacity to love. This gratitude does not seek recognition; it quietly fuels our ongoing journey of solidarity and care.

In the unfolding days ahead, we commit to walking this path together: to nurture newborns, support parents, and sustain the whole community with compassion and attentiveness. We trust that in each tender feeding and each shared story, we participate in a larger movement of beloved strength, where love overcomes isolation and resilience arises through mutual belonging.

May the presence of these newest lives inspire you to embrace hospitality in your own context—remembering that to welcome another is to welcome a spark of divine promise. In doing so, we join in a timeless flow: strangers become neighbors, neighbors become friends, and together we witness new life flourishing amid uncertainty.

At the Threshold
How might you foster "beloved strength" through small, consistent acts of welcome and care—especially when you face fragility or uncertainty in others or within yourself?

Antonella's Journey

Antonella carries with her a vibrant spirit that colors every room she enters. Growing up in South America, one of ten siblings, her early life was marked by both the lively rhythms of family and the challenges of a temperamental mother. Yet, through it all, Antonella found refuge and joy in soccer, poetry, and singing — the gifts that nurtured her soul.

In high school, a teacher opened her eyes to the world beyond her immediate surroundings, introducing her to geography and cultures far away. From that moment, the dream of a future in the United States or Canada took root deep within her.

After finishing high school, Antonella fulfilled her duty by serving in her country's military. When she was 22, she set out carefully to follow the path she had planned toward the U.S. But the journey was not without hardship. Along the way, Antonella endured a profound trauma—

assaulted by five men—which left her with an unplanned pregnancy. Though such an event might have crushed the hopes of many, Antonella's determination only grew stronger.

She arrived at Casa Alterna carrying not just a small bundle of new life—a baby girl born into our community—but also a fierce hope to heal and rebuild. Her spirit was unbroken.

Antonella's heart looks forward: she dreams of returning to work once she receives temporary protection status, continuing her education, and becoming a voice for women who have suffered violence. At Casa Alterna, she cherishes the English classes that help her navigate a new language and culture, and the simple pleasure of walking through Atlanta's green spaces, hand in hand with her daughter and friends.

For Antonella, community is more than just a group of people living under one roof—it is a shared existence, a mutual care that carries us through even the darkest times.

"Community means supporting each other," she says. "We're not just isolated individuals living in our own bubbles. We are multiple people in a shared bubble. When someone needs something, others step in to help, and the same is true in reverse."

This shared bubble is what sustains Antonella and her daughter as they move forward—step by step—toward healing and new beginnings. It is a testament to the deep human truth that none of us walks alone.

At the Threshold
How can you hold space for others in your community so that no one feels isolated in their pain or struggle?

MARCH TO JUNE 2024
Falling, Rising, and Finding Home

In early March 2024, while leading a walking tour of immigrant justice through the streets of Atlanta—tracing paths of witness and solidarity—I slipped and fell. The impact shattered my left humerus in several places. What began as a day of advocacy quickly became the start of a long and unexpected journey of healing, patience, and reflection.

On Good Friday, just weeks after the fall, I underwent surgery to repair the damage. As I was being prepared for anesthesia, half-joking and fully aware of the deeper symbolism of the day, I asked the anesthesiologist to assure me that I would rise again. That moment marked a poignant intersection between my physical brokenness and the spiritual truths I hold dear.

These chapters reflect that season—from the rawness of pain and vulnerability to the grace found in mutual hospitality and healing. The broken body I offered at the altar is both literal and metaphorical: a witness to the fragility and resilience we all carry. In the midst of this personal trial, I found myself drawing closer to the suffering of others—immigrants seeking refuge, families torn apart by violence, and those living under systems that too often break bodies and spirits alike.

May this story of falling and rising remind us that our wounds—personal and collective—can become gateways to compassion, solidarity, and ultimately, home.

This Is My Broken Body

On a Sunday morning, I stood at the altar, holding the bread and speaking words I had said countless times before: "This is my Body, broken for you." But this time, my voice trembled. My left arm was bound in a sling, my shoulder fractured in several places. Without planning, I added quietly, "And this is my broken body, too—offered in compassion and solidarity with all who suffer unjustly, especially our neighbors seeking refuge."

It had been just weeks since I fell while leading a walking vigil through the streets of Atlanta. We were tracing a path of witness for immigrant justice—passing places where immigrants suffer and symbols of power—when I slipped and struck my head and shoulder against a metal inverted cone encasing a solitary tree. My humerus shattered. This marked the beginning of a daunting journey of recovery.

I've lived long enough to know pain is not rare. Yet

this pain surprised me—with its sharpness, persistence, and the humility of depending on others for the simplest tasks. I had gone out to speak of freedom, only to find myself bound—by a sling, by weakness, by my own fragile flesh.

And yet, in that fragility, something sacred stirred.

As I sit, uncomfortable and healing at home, my thoughts reach far beyond my injury. I think of a child buried under rubble in Gaza who might also need surgery—but has no access to medical care because the local hospital has been bombed. I think of families fleeing violence, crossing borders with bodies and spirits crushed by trauma and oppression, searching for refuge. I think of Alejandro Hernandez and Dorlian Castillo, immigrant laborers in Baltimore whose lives were lost when the Francis Scott Key Bridge collapsed. Their names, their stories, broke something open in me.

Pain, when we allow it, can become a bridge—not just to others' suffering but to deeper solidarity. It can shatter illusions of control and comfort, awakening us to truths we'd rather not face. Sometimes that's the face of the wounded Christ. Sometimes it's the face of a stranger knocking on our door, asking for shelter.

My injury forced me to slow down, but it also deepened my resolve. I don't believe suffering is inherently redemptive—too many theologies have sanctified harm without confronting its causes. But I do believe that, if we listen closely, our suffering can shape us into people more willing to stand alongside the vulnerable and challenge the systems that keep them there.

The sling around my shoulder is a daily reminder: of

my body's limits, of my need for community, and of the call to remain tenderhearted in a world too quick to harden. It reminds me that we are most whole not when we are strong, but when we are honest about our wounds—and willing to see the wounds of others as sacred, too.

At the Threshold
When have you experienced your own vulnerability as a doorway to deeper empathy?

Find a Way Home

The words of Jacob Collier, sung alongside Brandi Carlile, echoed through my dim apartment during one of the harder seasons of my life—words that felt more like a prayer than a lyric:

> *Don't be afraid of the dark in your heart,*
> *you're gonna find a way*
> *to carry the weight of the world on your shoulders,*
> *you're gonna find a way home.*

In those weeks, I didn't just hear those words. I lived them.

Recovering from a shattered shoulder bone—my proximal humerus fractured in four places—was more than physical. It plunged me into deep discomfort, sleepless nights, and an unexpected vulnerability I could not push through or outrun. Surgery came. Plates and screws were placed to reconstruct what had broken. Then began the slow, humbling process of healing.

And in the midst of all this—still in pain, still sleeping upright in a recliner—there was hospitality.

I continued to receive guests in my home: three South American couples seeking asylum, including a family with two small children. My role looked different in that season. There were no long conversations around a table, no spontaneous outings. But the door stayed open. Meals were shared. Stories passed between us. And something remarkable happened: though I was the one offering them refuge, these new friends became a source of comfort to me. In their presence, I was reminded that vulnerability is not weakness—it is what allows us to touch grace.

They accepted me just as I was: bandaged, tired, and far from the energetic host I wanted to be. They saw me not as broken, but as human. They responded with gentleness and warmth. Their children's laughter filled the meetinghouse with light. Their quiet prayers lifted me. Their resilience mirrored my own slow return toward wholeness.

In welcoming others, I was being welcomed too.

Casa Alterna's vision of radical hospitality is not sustained by any one person. My injury taught me that deeply. As I healed, others kept the doors open, the meals warm, the prayers whispered, and the house full of laughter and light. Hospitality, I've come to know, is always a shared labor of love. Even when I could not lift my own arm, I was being held.

In seasons when I can give freely and in seasons when I can barely lift my own arm, the spirit of welcome continues. Not because of me, but because hospitality was never meant to be a solo act. It lives in the threshold between guest and host, in the quiet exchange of presence, in the sacred space where we are seen and received—just as we are.

You're gonna find a way home.

At the Threshold
When have you experienced welcome not as something you offered, but something you received—perhaps in a season when you had little to give?

TRUMP 2.0
Hospitality as Resistance

Since Donald Trump's re-election for a second term, his promise of mass deportations has unfolded into a harsh campaign of terror against immigrants and asylum seekers. Detention centers are overflowing, families continue to be torn apart, and fear deepens.

In this moment of rising authoritarian repression and brutal harshness, Casa Alterna has pivoted to meet the urgent needs of vulnerable immigrants in new ways. One such pivot is Compas at the Gates—our ongoing accompaniment outside the ICE field office in Atlanta—we gather not as caseworkers, fixers, or heroes, but as companions. We come with know-your-rights cards, food, information, and open hearts. We stand with those facing a system designed to erase them, choosing radical hospitality as an act of resistance.

Like the midwives who refused to obey Pharaoh's orders, our work of welcoming, sheltering, and standing alongside the vulnerable remains a living and growing form of defiance. We continue to choose love over fear, solidarity over silence, building communities of welcome when exclusion and violence seek to prevail.

This is a call to stand at the threshold—to embody tenderness in a hardened world—and to join in building something brave and new, here and now.

Ending Political Violence Begins with Welcome

"There is no place in America for this kind of violence. It's sick. It's sick."
— President Joe Biden

During a political rally in Pennsylvania, a man opened fire as former President Donald Trump gave a campaign speech. The bullet missed killing him, but not by much—it grazed his ear as he turned to look at a chart behind him. The chart, as it happens, was filled with anti-immigrant claims, asserting that the Southern border is flooded with "prisoners, terrorists, and people from mental institutions."

That chart, intended to stoke fear, became a shield. The irony isn't lost on me.

As I watched the news coverage and listened to both President Biden's condemnation of the violence and Trump's retelling of his narrow escape, I found myself reflecting on the ways political violence manifests—

not just in dramatic acts of gunfire, but in quieter, more insidious ways. I thought about the asylum seekers sleeping peacefully in the transitional housing offered through our community. I thought about the language used to describe them, and how that language—no matter how coded or casual—can be deadly, too.

Violence is more than bullets.

Theologian Walter Wink skillfully dismantled the myth of redemptive violence—the belief that violence saves, that it is the final solution, the last defense of justice. Wink's challenge was simple but radical: Violence cannot heal us. In his words, "the myth of redemptive violence is the primary spiritual problem in our world."

I've come to believe this, not just intellectually, but in my bones.

And yet our culture, particularly our political discourse, continues to glorify violence: in words, in policy, in the spectacle of power. At that Pennsylvania rally, the chart—meant to incite fear about immigrants—was not merely part of the backdrop. It was part of the problem. The same rhetoric that demonizes the stranger also fuels policies that deny them safety, food, or the right to work. It allows us to imagine that some people are less than human.

This is violence, too.

The late David Gil, a Holocaust survivor turned social work scholar, once defined violence as anything that prevents a person from achieving their full human potential. His definition stretches us. It demands that we recognize violence not just in bombs or bullets, but in border policies, in hunger, in the deliberate withholding of dignity.

It reminds me of Venezuela—the home country of many of our guests. Arbitrary detentions. Political repression. Medical collapse. Mass displacement. This isn't just mismanagement; it is structural violence, reinforced by the international community's apathy and the Venezuelan government's cruelty. And the effects of that violence ripple outward—right to our doorstep.

So what does it mean to respond nonviolently?

For me, the answer begins in the form of an open door and a made-up bed. It's a quiet welcome whispered across language barriers and bureaucratic red tape. It's legal accompaniment and cups of coffee, shared meals and rides to immigration court. It's refusing to mirror the cruelty that so many of our guests have endured. It's knowing that policy must be challenged, yes—but also that a single act of hospitality can confront violence at its root: the lie that someone is unworthy of love.

Nonviolence does not mean passivity. It means resistance rooted in dignity.

And that includes holding our leaders accountable—not just the ones we disagree with. It includes challenging President Biden's policies when they inflict harm, such as capping the number of asylum seekers processed each day or funding deportation efforts abroad. If we're serious about nonviolence, we must be willing to call out violence, even when it wears the clothes of moderation.

But we must also go deeper—into the roots of our culture's fascination with domination. The reports about the would-be assassin of Trump noted that he had been bullied in school. That doesn't excuse the act. But it does point to a deeper wound. Our society nurtures violence in our homes, our schools, our speech. Until we confront this culture of humiliation, we will continue to see its violent fruit.

At Casa Alterna, we respond with what we call radical hospitality. Not because it's a catchy phrase, but because it's how we survive. We host families and individuals seeking asylum. Many stay in our transitional house for months. They are not "invaders." They are human beings looking for safety, healing, and the freedom to dream again.

Hospitality is not a political strategy. It is a spiritual discipline.

I believe that real safety will not come from higher walls or crueler policies. It will come when we disarm our fear. When we tell the truth about injustice. When we reject the myth that someone must be punished in order for others to be safe. When we make space—for strangers and for stories.

We can't end violence with more violence. But we can make it harder for violence to take root by offering another way.

A way of presence.
A way of welcome.
A way of peace.

At the Threshold
What forms of violence have you been taught to accept as "necessary" or "normal"?

Radical Hospitality as Resistance

"I zoom out further to the lifespans of trees and rocks, heading into spiritual reminders that nothing lasts forever."
— Daniel Hunter

Daniel Hunter's words invite us to step back from immediate fears and anxieties to see a larger spiritual horizon. While systems of oppression rise and fall like passing storms, our commitment to love and sanctuary endures—rooted deep, like ancient trees and stones growing steadfast in the soil of hope.

When the world feels harsh and uncertain—especially for immigrants and those living on the margins—I return again and again to these steady rhythms of nature and spirit. Trees stand for centuries; rocks endure for millennia. They remind me that the storms we face will pass, that no fear or force is eternal. Yet the way we respond to those storms—how we show up for one another—shapes the arc of healing and hope.

Fear and division thrive on isolation and suspicion. Authoritarianism feeds on distrust, and distrust breeds loneliness. But the work of radical hospitality depends on trust—trust in ourselves, in each other, and in the Spirit that moves through us all. This trust is the foundation for sanctuary: communities that hold space for healing, resistance, and belonging.

Hospitality is more than opening a door or offering shelter. It is an act of love that defies borders, challenges systems of exclusion, and proclaims a different story—that every person deserves dignity, safety, and welcome. When we gather around tables, in homes, in meeting rooms, we build something holy—something no law or policy can fully control or undo.

This work calls for discernment. Not every crisis demands our immediate action, and we cannot pour from an empty cup. Listening deeply—to our own limits, to the needs of those we serve, and to the guidance of our communities—helps us sustain this work over time. It invites us to focus where our love and presence can truly make a difference.

At the heart of this resistance is a commitment to protect and nurture those whom the world often tries to push aside. Creating spaces where families find safety, where children are shielded from fear, where stories of trauma meet care instead of judgment—this is our call. It means walking alongside each other through hard moments and celebrating small victories that remind us a more beautiful world is possible.

In the face of rising challenges, we hold fast to the belief that love is stronger than hate, that community is stronger than isolation, and that hospitality is a radical act of defiance and hope. Together, we build sanctuaries—not just physical places, but communities of mutual support and belonging—that carry us through uncertain times.

At the Threshold
What does it mean for you to trust love enough to build a community that welcomes the vulnerable?

Midwives of Justice: A Call for Sanctuary

In the book of Exodus, two women—Shiphrah and Puah—were called midwives, but they were much more than birth attendants. They were midwives of justice. When Pharaoh commanded them to kill every newborn boy, they chose instead to protect life, defying oppressive power with quiet but fierce courage. Their faith led them to act with love and resistance in the face of fear and cruelty.

Today, we find ourselves called to a similar role. Our world faces its own Pharaohs—systems and leaders who use fear to justify tearing families apart and denying sanctuary to those seeking safety. But just as Shiphrah and Puah stood for life and justice, so too must we rise up as midwives of justice, offering sanctuary, protection, and radical hospitality to our neighbors who are vulnerable and in need.

WELCOME, FRIENDS

In 2025, political division hardened into a climate of fear and suspicion. Leaders stoked anxieties about immigrants, casting them as threats to jobs, safety, and the nation's future. Harsh policies tore families apart—detaining boys, stripping citizenship, breaking the bonds that hold people together.

But in the face of this cruelty, a quiet and powerful resistance arose. Rooted in faith and justice, people across the country opened their doors and their hearts. Like Shiphrah and Puah before them, they chose love over fear, protection over obedience to unjust commands.

"These people are too resourceful," they seemed to say. "By the time the authorities arrive, they've already found safety."

Communities of faith, activists, and immigrants united in nonviolent resistance—creating sanctuary spaces, raising their voices in protest, and building networks of care and solidarity.

This is our Shiphrah and Puah moment.

When faced with systems bent on oppression, when fear threatens to divide us, we are called to choose love, to resist injustice, and to protect the vulnerable. The courage of those midwives centuries ago offers us a model: to defy cruel commands, to listen to the voice of conscience, and to act with unwavering faith.

At the Threshold
In what ways is God calling you to be a modern-day Shiphrah or Puah, standing with the vulnerable and choosing love over fear?

No Way Back Home

Part One of a Lenten Reflection

Lent beckons into the wilderness—not just a wilderness of sand and thorny bushes, but a realm of the soul. Of testing. A place where the noise of the world falls away and we come face to face with both our vulnerability and the unjust systems that shape our lives.

In the Gospel story, we encounter Jesus in this wilderness: hungry, vulnerable, solitary—yet resolute. He stands defiant in the face of forces bent on crushing his spirit and compromising his calling.

The wilderness strips away our comforting illusions. It compels us to confront who we are and what we stand for. It shines a stark light on the Powers that govern our world and dares us to resist them—not just on behalf of ourselves, but on behalf of all who suffer beneath their weight.

For me, that wilderness is not only metaphorical.

It's made of concrete, metal, and glass—manifested in places like the field office of Immigration and Customs Enforcement (ICE) in downtown Atlanta. It's there that I often stand, alongside volunteers from Court Compas, offering presence and solidarity to those made most vulnerable by a merciless immigration system.

And it's there, in the shadow of that brutal machinery, that I recently met two Venezuelan men whose story has stayed with me.

A Story of Two Venezuelan Men

The cousins approached me with a quiet desperation. They were not looking to stay in the United States; they were hoping to find a way back home. They had done everything they were supposed to do—followed the rules, attended check-ins, complied with the system. But one of them had made a simple, honest mistake: in the disorienting process of building a life in a foreign land, he had failed to update his address with immigration authorities. As a result, he never received notice of his court date. There are no public defenders in immigration court, no guide to help navigate the maze. He missed the hearing. His absence triggered an automatic deportation order.

Now, with no legal recourse and no clear path back to Venezuela, they stood outside ICE headquarters, asking to be deported.

One of the men showed me a photo of his wife and daughter, still in Venezuela. The ache in his voice was unmistakable. He was willing to endure anything—detention, shackles, humiliation—just for a chance to hold them again. But the path he sought was uncertain and dangerous. Without proper documentation or a consulate willing to assist, they were trapped in a bureaucratic no man's land, with no way forward and no way back.

This system does not merely fail people. It entraps them. It criminalizes migration and punishes the desperate. It functions much like the Pharaoh of old: hardening its heart, pressuring people to betray one another, and punishing those who dare to seek safety—or to offer it.

Jesus in the Wilderness

Scripture tells us that Jesus, too, was led into the wilderness. And there he faced three profound temptations:

"Turn these stones into bread."
A lure to choose comfort over integrity, to exchange dignity for mere survival.

"Throw yourself down, and the angels will catch you."
A dare to prove oneself through spectacle, to demand validation on the world's terms.

"Bow to me, and I will give you all the kingdoms of the world."
An offer of seductive power—security in exchange for allegiance.

Are these not the same temptations faced by migrants and those who stand in solidarity with them today?

The pressure to trade integrity for a meal or a bed. The urge to prove worthiness in a system built on exclusion. The temptation to compromise just enough to stay safe.

But Jesus resists.

He does not weaponize divine power to escape suffering. He does not bend to the logic of empire. He chooses the harder way—the Way of Love—and in doing so, he exposes the Powers for what they are: fragile, fearful, and ultimately false.

As one preacher wryly noted, "But-ology may be the highest form of theology." But Jesus resisted. But he chose love. But he stood firm.

In his steadfast defiance, Jesus invites us to do the same. He invites us into the wilderness not to break us—but to remake us. To see clearly. To resist bravely. To prepare our hearts to follow him into the Beloved Community.

And so, standing beside two men caught in the wilderness of the immigration system, and beside a Savior who walks with the suffering, I find the question not whether the wilderness is real—it is—but what we will choose while we're in it.

Will we be tempted to turn away, to shield ourselves from suffering and injustice? Or will we stay present, grounded, and courageous?

The wilderness is real, and the question lingers—not whether to turn away, but how to stand firm when the way is hard. That day outside the ICE field office, I found myself wrestling with more than just their story. I wondered: what does it truly mean to walk this Way of Love when hope feels so fragile?

At the Threshold
What does it truly mean to walk the Way of Love when hope feels so fragile?

Love is the Way Home

Part two of a Lenten reflection

Their faces, their quiet desperation, stayed with me. As the cousins stood before the imposing ICE field office, asking to be deported, I was forced to confront my own complicity—was my presence enough? Could I do more? The weight of the moment pressed hard, and I reached out for guidance.

One of the men had unknowingly sealed his fate with a simple mistake—he had moved, and in the disorienting shuffle of trying to build a life in a new country, failed to update his address with immigration authorities. Because of this, he never received notice of his court hearing. There are no public defenders provided to immigrants in removal proceedings—no one to guide them through the confusing and unforgiving bureaucratic process. He missed the hearing, and his absence resulted in an automatic deportation order. Stripped of options, the cousins came to

ICE with a desperate request: to turn themselves in, hoping that deportation might finally bring them home.

Their request outside the goliath ICE field office made me wrestle with my own inner temptations. Was my intervention enough—or was I complicit? When they told me they wanted to ask ICE to deport them, I laid out the grim realities: indefinite detention, hardship and suffering, a humiliating, shackled deportation—sometimes to a land not even their own—and a future cloaked in uncertainty. In the urgency of their plight, I reached out to a trusted immigration attorney who shared these concerns. Together, we believed the men were making an informed, though agonizing, choice. With no assured way back home, I watched as they chose to surrender—the one with the deportation order detained, the other released.

Reflecting on this moment, I recognize a few truths clearly. My calling is one of solidarity, not saviorism. I am here to offer small acts of great love, not to topple giants disguised as institutions.

But I also must confess: I missed opportunities. I could have invited them back for deeper discernment. I could have recorded the detained man's identification number for follow-up. I might have sought the wisdom of a friend who has lived in the shadows of undocumented life for decades—a well of resilience and hope.

Lent calls us to face our fragility, to remember that we are dust. But it is not a season for self-pity or paralysis. It is a time to resolve to act with greater compassion and courage.

If Jesus teaches us anything from the wilderness, it

is this: true greatness is not wielded by power or authority. It is not found in bending to empire or fear.

Greatness comes from standing firm in the Way of Love—resisting the seduction of compromise even when the cost is high.

So I ask myself—and I invite you to ask yourself—how will we respond when confronted with the struggles of vulnerable immigrants yearning for dignity? Will we stand against systems that exclude and oppress, or will we allow complicity to take root?

What does it mean to embody the Way of Love in our daily lives, especially when it demands sacrifice and discomfort?

The path of hospitality and justice leads us repeatedly into the wilderness. But we do not walk alone. We journey with the Spirit, with one another, remembering Jesus and the countless others who have walked this difficult road before us.

At the Threshold
What does it mean to embody the Way of Love, especially when it demands sacrifice and discomfort?

Defiant Thanks at the Gates

Most mornings, as the city begins its restless hum, we gather at the gates of Immigration and Customs Enforcement—a place marked not by welcome, but by watchfulness and waiting. Here stand newcomers to this land, clutching paperwork, whispering prayers, or simply holding the hands of loved ones, bracing themselves for what lies ahead.

We come with simple tools: Know-Your-Rights cards, bags of snacks, and open hearts. Our role is to stand alongside them—to inform, to encourage, to offer hospitality where we can, and to witness the unfolding story of hope amid hardship. This is accompaniment in its rawest form: showing up at the gates of a system designed to intimidate, but refusing to be broken by it.

One morning, I met a man from Mexico, fasting and praying while his wife and child checked in inside. His quiet vigil was an act of faith in the face of desperation. When his family emerged, relief softened his worn face.

"God has answered my prayers," he said softly. Then, turning to his young son, he asked, "Please, sing a song of thanks."

The boy's small voice rose, pure and steady, cutting through the tension like a light in a dark room. Even the traffic seemed to pause, and the murmurs hushed as his song floated outside the gates built to break spirits.

Demos gracias al Señor, demos gracias... (We give thanks to the Lord, we give thanks...)

This place, with its towering gates, armed guards, and layers of surveillance, is meant to intimidate. But what we witnessed there was something else entirely. We saw love, hope, and the unbreakable spirit of a family determined to stay together.

Later that day, a man from the Caribbean arrived in Atlanta early for his immigration court date. He had no place to stay and no money for lodging. A woman nearby, selling comfort food from her car, noticed his unease and pointed him toward us. Without hesitation, we welcomed him into Casa Alterna—no strings attached, no questions asked—just a safe place to rest his head and soul.

Hospitality is what mercy looks like in practice. It is never transactional. It is a radical invitation: no one should ever face the unknown alone. In this strange land, we say, we will be your friend.

Another morning brought news that filled my heart with quiet joy. A West African man, after years of reporting to ICE, told me this would be his last day. His asylum had been granted, and his green card was on the way. His family's future was finally secure, and for the first time, he felt free.

He introduced me to his wife and child standing beside him, their faces touched by the crisp Atlanta air. And as if in unison, he repeated the words I had heard before on that very sidewalk:

"We give thanks."

These gates, built to inspire fear and division, become the backdrop for something far greater: mercy rooted in community, resilience that refuses to be crushed, and a hope that cannot be silenced.

We give thanks.

At the Threshold
How can showing up and simply bearing witness transform a moment or a life?

Standing in Love, Not Fear

Most weekday mornings, just as the sun lifts over downtown Atlanta, a small circle of us gathers outside the grey, looming walls of the immigration court and ICE field office. We do not come with banners. We do not shout. We simply stand—with open hearts, soft eyes, and sometimes a thermos of coffee—offering presence and witness to those navigating the cruel machinery of immigration enforcement.

This steadfast presence—standing together with those navigating the system—is more than a gesture of support. It is a circle of mutual care, where we hold each other's stories, share silences, and make space for grief and grace alike. In that shared space, the boundaries between helper and helped blur, and we discover how much we need one another.

On any given morning, you might find someone like me paired with a retired teacher, a grad student, or a grandmother from the neighborhood. Some of us speak

Spanish fluently. Others fumble lovingly with the words. All of us are learning.

I remember a morning when a father and his teenage son exited the building after a favorable check-in. They had arrived tense and quiet. But as they emerged, they were laughing—the boy tossing his hands in the air like he'd just won something invisible. In a way, he had. Relief had been granted. Time had been given. Hope, if only briefly, was allowed to bloom.

Other moments are heavier.

Like Cinthia.

Nineteen. Six months pregnant. She came alone to her ICE check-in—and didn't walk back out. The next morning, a friend and his mother came searching for her. Her name wasn't on any public list. We knew what that meant. We still hold her and the child she carries in the Light, trusting that our partners may reach her in detention, that she may feel—somehow—that she is not forgotten.

Some of us write small reflections after our shifts. One person wrote, "What I expected was fear. What I saw was patience. Maybe because fear has become a part of their daily lives." Another wrote, "I just let my heart listen." And someone else, still moved days later, said, "Every encounter was sacred. Every story changed me."

One morning, a little boy named Emanuel—eight years old—became someone's Spanish teacher as they waited. Another day, a volunteer gently helped a man who had been tricked out of parking money. There are days when mothers whisper their worries through tears: "I don't let my son play outside. I'm always afraid."

We listen.

We do not fix. We do not save. But we do stand with.

And in a world that so often wants to forget, dismiss, or detain, standing with someone can be a quiet kind of miracle.

These moments—small as they may seem—are not charity. They are resistance rooted in love. They are communion in the shadow of empire. They are our humble attempt to echo the truth that every person is beloved, and no one should walk through fear alone.

At the Threshold

In your own community, where might you show up—not to fix or solve, but simply to stand in love, listen with your heart, and remind someone they are not alone?

Beloved, Not Exceptional

"But the midwives feared God; they did not do as the king of Egypt commanded them."
Exodus 1:17 (NRSV)

In the shadow of 9/11, something shifted in the soul of the nation—and in our sanctuaries. The church I attended, which had long rejected icons, suddenly raised the American flag above the congregation. No cross. No Christ. Just the Stars and Stripes, hoisted where the cross should have been all along.

It was a disorienting moment. A signal. As if our collective grief had been quietly repurposed—not into communal healing, but into national myth. Compassion surrendered to control. Lament was replaced by allegiance.

This is what American exceptionalism does. It doesn't simply elevate the nation—it sanctifies it. It weaves together conquest, capitalism, racism, and militarism into a civil religion, baptizing empire and dressing Caesar in the robes of Christ. And when that mythology is questioned, the response is rarely repentance. Instead, freedom becomes a threat. Dissent becomes disloyalty. We see it in the rise of surveillance, in indefinite detention, in the criminalization of migration, and in the scapegoating of the vulnerable.

Empires don't just thrive on power. They thrive on forgetting.

They are sustained by the stories we refuse to remember: the genocide of Indigenous peoples, the theft of their lands, the chattel slavery of Africans upheld by a theology that proclaimed white supremacy as divine design. This historical amnesia is no accident. It is the privilege of the powerful—a weapon used to silence those whose memory threatens the narrative.

Scripture tells us every generation has its Pharaohs—rulers who weaponize fear to tighten their grip. Pharaoh, fearing the growing number of foreigners in Egypt, transformed his fear into policy. He enslaved the Israelites, turning their labor into profit and their presence into a "problem." His cruelty was cloaked in national interest.

Sound familiar?

Today, Venezuelans are deported to inhumane prisons. Asylum seekers are diverted to Guantanamo. Migrants languish in privately run detention centers where human pain is converted into corporate revenue. This is not a failure of the system—it is the system working as designed. From Japanese internment to the Muslim ban, from the Trail of Tears to the border wall, America has long relied on scapegoats to serve its myth.

And yet, another story has always run alongside this one.

Dr. King called it the Beloved Community—not a utopia, but a vision rooted in memory, humility, and moral courage. A society where justice and reconciliation embrace. A people who refuse to forget—and in their remembering, begin to repair. "The aftermath of nonviolence is the creation of the beloved community," King wrote. "The aftermath of violence is tragic bitterness."

This vision is not sentimental. It is subversive. It dares us to confront national myth with truth, to interrupt fear with solidarity, and to build relationships empire cannot co-opt.

At Casa Alterna, I've seen glimpses of this. The Beloved Community is not grand or headline-worthy. It is small, slow, and sacred. It looks like accompanying a mother through deportation proceedings. It looks like praying outside detention centers, holding vigil with families, offering a place to rest. It lives in the joyful resistance of those who—despite displacement and despair—share meals, swap stories, and hold fast to hope. The Beloved Community isn't a program. It's a posture.

I see it in those who show up outside ICE—not for performance, but for presence. In the family of Alma Bowman, who demand both her release and the redemption of the nation's soul. In teachers who advocate for children standing alone before immigration judges. In undocumented neighbors who care for one another long before any system ever will.

And I see it in the midwives of Exodus. They didn't

organize a revolution. They simply refused to comply. They saved lives—not by toppling power, but by resisting its cruelty. Their defiance was quiet. But it was holy.

That is the invitation before us now.

The rise of authoritarianism draped in patriotism is real. So is the resistance. And it begins with remembering. With refusing to forget the stories empire wants erased. With choosing solidarity over safety. With practicing love as disobedience.

Migration will not stop. Climate collapse, political violence, and greed will continue to uproot lives. But our response need not be fear. It can be welcome. It can be faith. It can be midwifed by mercy.

The Beloved Community is not beyond reach. It lives wherever we remember rightly, refuse complicity, and let love carry us across borders—geographic, political, and spiritual.

As Gandhi reminded us, "There have been tyrants and murderers, and for a time, they can seem invincible. But in the end, they always fall. Always."

The invitation remains:

Don't bow. Build.

Don't forget. Remember.

Don't despair. Love.

At the Threshold

In your own community, what myths need to be unlearned—and what memories need to be reclaimed—in order to live more fully into the Beloved Community?

Mary, Don't You Weep

"Oh, Mary, don't you weep. Oh, Martha, don't you moan…"

This week, I saw Mary weep.

Not the Mary in Scriptures who stood at her brother's tomb, but Mary the food vendor, weeping for those detained outside the gates of a federal immigration facility. For years now, she has served warm food by the curb of this building, its concrete worn by the footsteps of the damned, the desperate, and the devoted. This place has become her place of constant care and simple hospitality.

But something has changed. She says it has never felt this cruel.

She has noticed the detention vans leaving more frequently now. Just last week, a man with a heart condition left the building clutching his next appointment slip. He sat down beside her car, exhausted, having forgotten to take his medication. While resting and eating her food, he was suddenly taken back into custody, presumably headed to an immigration detention center, right there in front of Mary.

This week, Mary had stepped inside the building to use the restroom when a woman stumbled out, shell-shocked and sobbing, clinging to a loved one's belt like it was the last piece of him she might ever hold. He had been taken. I saw her too, one of the moaning Marthas, undone by grief, crying into the open air with no one to answer. I walked beside her, but she wasn't ready to receive consolation, not from a stranger. Then Mary emerged behind her, also weeping. She let me walk with her to her usual place behind her car and simply listen.

Mary's eyes have seen too much. Her heart is overwhelmed.

She wonders, "Why are so many good people suffering?"

The cruelty is crescendoing. It is there in the tears, the belts, and the vans.

These are heavy days. If immigrant families and those who accompany them are to endure the years ahead, we must care for ourselves and one another with fierce tenderness. We must name the trauma and admit that even as we walk with others through their valleys, we are being wounded too.

Casa Alterna's volunteers and staff are not immune to compassion fatigue and vicarious trauma.

We might notice a restless urge to fix, to solve, or to stay constantly busy.

We might hear teammates express feelings of not doing enough, even when they are giving their all.

I find myself napping most afternoons, always feeling behind on the rest of my work.

Sometimes, I feel the pressure to have answers for every crisis, as if certainty could ease the pain.

These responses are natural. They show how deeply we care and how much this work touches us.

This is not a struggle we win with haste or force. It is a calling to steadfast presence, where love becomes our measure and truth our guide.

A volunteer and I recently reflected on this work of accompaniment as a kind of hospice care, tending to those facing deeply painful transitions with dignity and presence. Statistically, the prognosis may be grim. The systems may seem immovable. But that does not make our work futile. It makes it sacred.

And the sacred is not a place of certainty but of mystery. It is a place where agency and dignity can be reclaimed against all odds. Where an interior liberty can free even the most oppressed soul from the shackles of fear. Much of the world knows this. Most people on this planet live with uncertainty. The courage of those we accompany calls us not to pity but to reverence.

We are witnesses to redemption seeking to redefine our history. The deeper we listen to the stories and sorrows of our modern-day Marys and Marthas, the more we break and the more we are invited to unmask our privilege and choose a life of solidarity. The question for us is: In that breaking, will we allow more light and love to get through the cracks?

Harriet Tubman, Clara Barton, Oscar Romero, and a

long line of ancestors are still singing. Can you hear them? They're singing over us. Singing through us. Singing to Mary, and to every one of us whose hearts are raw from bearing witness:

"Pharaoh's army got drowned in the Red Sea. Oh, Mary, don't you weep."

One day, though we do not know when, the empires will fall.

The silence of complicity will give way. And justice will roll down like waters and righteousness like an ever-flowing stream.

Until then, we take heart in this:

Outside these gates, we witness a convergence of the wretched and despised from every corner of the world. Each morning they arrive, carrying fear, yes, but even more carrying hope.

They are a stream of living water,

Flowing through despair,

Washing over cruelty,

Carving a way, drop by drop, toward a more beautiful world.

"Pharaoh's army got drowned in the Red Sea. Oh, Mary, don't you weep."

At the Threshold

How are you tending to your own heart as you accompany others through suffering—and what helps you keep singing through the sorrow?

Compas at the Gates

"Love is the work of mirroring and magnifying each other's light."
—James Baldwin

What if the truest form of resistance is simply to remain tender in a hardened world?

There's a stretch of concrete outside Atlanta's ICE field office that I've come to know by heart. The sun rises there just like anywhere else, but what happens on that sidewalk feels unlike anywhere else I've ever stood. We gather—not as caseworkers or counselors, not as fixers, and certainly not as heroes—but as companions. Compas.

We come with know-your-rights cards, breakfast bars, information about free accommodations, and open hearts. That's all. And some days, it's enough. Not to solve the crisis. But to stay human within it.

Some who join us arrive nervous, unsure of what

to say or how to help. I remember Mariana—her first day, she hovered close, shadowing me as I moved down the line of families waiting to enter the building. By morning's end, she had found her own rhythm: quietly translating, gently offering resources, standing in solidarity. That's how accompaniment begins. Presence begets courage. Solidarity takes root, one tender act at a time.

Emma once helped a Haitian man, Jean, complete a form—simple to some, a labyrinth to him. He tried to pay her. She kindly declined. In that moment, I saw the contrast so clearly: the transactional world we've been taught to expect, and the counter-economy we're trying to create. One not based on earning, but on being. Not on debt, but on dignity.

Cindy, steady and quiet, was greeted by name by our unhoused neighbors. Others return, week after week, moved by something deeper than duty.

Even the parking lot across the street has become a front in our quiet resistance. Advising newcomers to park a few blocks away—saving over ten dollars—may seem trivial. But when you're already being bled by a system built on extraction, every dollar matters. Every act of protection—of naming dignity—is resistance.

Alberto—unflinching and kind—stood his ground when the parking lot manager shouted at us. "They may get angry," he said in his trademark Italian accent, "but at least we tell the truth."

Still, not every moment is heavy. One morning, a mother and daughter approached the building, visibly tired from their pre-dawn journey. As we began talking, I learned they were from La Libertad, Guatemala—the very town where Charlotte and I once lived for six weeks. It's a place where Casa Alterna has built deep relationships and collaborative initiatives over the years. The mother, Rosa, smiled with recognition as we named mutual friends. Her daughter, Lucía, attends the school where Charlotte once taught. We snapped a picture to send to her English teacher, Ms. Aldridge. A flash of grace in a space too often marked by fear.

And sometimes, the needs that meet us at the gates are vast. A couple approached me once, asking for help to return to their home country. They had tried to self-deport—ICE turned them away. They had nowhere to go. I invited them to the meetinghouse, where they stayed nearly two weeks. Together, with trusted partners, we helped them return home with dignity.

All of this is holy accompaniment. Not directing or rescuing, but walking alongside people in motion. Responding with presence, not performance. Staying close to those who carry both fear and hope.

It's hard to describe what happens in those hours at the gates of ICE. There are no headlines, no loud declarations. We often don't feel like we prevail. But there are names remembered, eyes met, tears honored. There is sacred ground underfoot—not because of where we are, but because of how we are.

Outside these gates, we see systems designed to disappear people. But we choose to show up, name them, and stand with them.

Where ICE erases, we remember.

Where bureaucracies dehumanize, we affirm. Where despair tightens its grip, we offer a soft embrace. Love crosses borders. And on that sidewalk, morning after morning, we are building something tender and brave—a new world in the shell of the old.

As civil rights activist Vincent Harding reimagined the spiritual "We Are Climbing Jacob's Ladder," he reminded us:

> *We are building up a new world*
> *We are building up a new world*
> *We are building up a new world*
> *Builders must be strong!*

At the Threshold
In the midst of hardship and uncertainty, how might you choose to be a companion—offering presence, courage, and love—in your own community?

Epilogue: Carry On, The Welcome Never Ends

When I first met Sarah Jackson, she was a wide-eyed young woman full of hope and determination. She had traveled all the way from Colorado to Georgia, eager to learn how to offer radical hospitality to immigrants detained far from home. Sarah wondered how, as one person—naive and inexperienced—she could possibly replicate the work that had taken a dedicated team years to build.

I shared with her a simple process—one that has guided me time and again:

- **Know your vision.** What is the spark in your soul—a picture of the future that feels urgent and alive?
- **Embody your vision.** Don't wait for permission or company. In the smallest way you can, incarnate that vision. Give it flesh and breath through your living.
- **Communicate your vision.** Share what you are

learning and living with honesty and invitation. A good testimony is a powerful lighthouse.

- **Watch what happens.** People—others like you—will appear, drawn by the hope and integrity of your work. As Gandhi's character says in the iconic 1982 film of the same name, "At first I was amazed... but when you are fighting in a just cause, people seem to pop up—like you—right out of the pavement."

Sarah took those words to heart. Back in Colorado, she rented a modest two-bedroom apartment next to an immigration detention facility and began volunteering—ironically, by teaching English to people in deportation proceedings. Soon, she was offering hospitality to newly liberated immigrants and to their families who had traveled great distances to reunite. Her small act of great love ignited a movement. What began as one apartment became a harbor of welcome. Her journey is now beautifully told in her book, *The House That Love Built: Why I Opened My Door to Immigrants and How We Found Hope Beyond a Broken System.* This book has been a witness to the power of welcome—the places where wounds meet grace, where strangers become friends, and where hope takes flesh. I have told these stories to invite you into that same sacred work. At the threshold of each chapter, you were invited to pause and ask yourself how radical hospitality might find its place in your life.

Sarah's story is just one reminder: when you act from love, you never act alone.

Radical hospitality isn't reserved for saints. As Dorothy Day said, "Don't call me a saint—I don't want to be dismissed so easily." This is the paradox of the story we have lived and shared here: everyone can offer small acts with great love. Perhaps only a few of us do so over and over, but those small acts, faithfully repeated, become the work of a lifetime—and the change the world needs.

This book has been a witness to the power of welcome—the places where wounds meet grace, where strangers become friends, and where hope takes flesh. I have told these stories to invite you into that same sacred work. At the threshold of each chapter, you were invited to pause and ask yourself how radical hospitality might find its place in your life.

Now, at this book's close, I invite you again:

What vision stirs within you for a more beautiful world?

In what small ways might you begin to embody welcome?

How might your story invite others into this sacred work?

You do not need a grand plan or perfect readiness. Begin with the small things—listening with presence, offering a meal, holding space for grief, or simply saying, "Welcome, Friends." Such acts widen the circle of our shared humanity.

And know this: you are not alone. The work of hospitality has been carried by countless others—those whose names we may never know but whose courage and love ripple through our lives like quiet blessings. Their footsteps guide us as we walk this path together.

May you find strength in vulnerability,
courage in presence,
and joy in welcome.

A Charge to Be A Refuge
(Inspired by Carrie Newcomer's song, Sanctuary)

May you be a refuge—
a steadfast haven in the storms around you.
May you keep the embers burning—
offering warmth when others' fires grow dim.
May you remember the small gestures—
the sprigs of rosemary—that bring healing and hope.
Be sanctuary for the weary,
a place where strength is restored,
so that those who come to you
can carry on,
carry on,
carry on.

The welcome never ends.

It lives in the spaces between us—in the stories we share, the wounds we touch, and the love we give.

Welcome, friends. Carry on.

Acknowledgments

Love, like this book, never travels alone. It moves across borders—of time, of place, of loss—and it carries with it the fingerprints of many. These are some of the hands that helped carry me.

First and foremost, I want to thank my wife, Charlotte. She is my anchor, my fiercest cheerleader, and the love that keeps me steady through every storm. She previewed this manuscript with a heart too full of faith in me to offer much critical feedback—but I treasure her belief all the same.

I owe a profound debt of gratitude to Shawn and Jen Casselberry, the editors and publishers of this, my inaugural book. Shawn's kindness and patience carried me through the hardest years. In 2016, when my youngest son Eli passed unexpectedly, I could not imagine finishing the book that Shawn and I had started together. We still haven't finished it. Yet Shawn never judged my grief; instead, he held space for me. In fact, he was the one who pointed out that my tenure as Friend-in-Residence, the resurrection of Casa Alterna, and my blog were a book six years in the making. He was right.

To my sons—without Jairo, there would be no Casa Alterna. His adoption at age two led us into a new life among immigrants and a reordered vision of family and hospitality. Now, you are nearly the age I was when we first welcomed you home. This book is a testament to my commitment to love you as best I know how. And Eli—this book is my promise to you. You once wrote that the difference between a writer and an author is simple: an author is published. Your mother and I have now posthumously published two of your books, written when you were twelve to fourteen years old. In my fifties, I join you as an author.

To everyone who has ever called Casa Alterna community, home, or place of work: I so appreciate the ways you have made me a better human. You lift my sometimes heavy arms and hold me up when I falter. And to Norma, a co-founder of Casa Alterna, who—without legal status or health insurance—died far too young from renal disease: you were my prophet. These are my stories, and they are your living witness.

I give thanks to the Atlanta Friends Meeting, who first welcomed me into what was only supposed to be a two-year stint as Friend-in-Residence. I am now nearing my seventh anniversary in that role. Clearly, as Quakers say, Way has opened for all of us. And to Atlanta Mennonite Church, thank you for your steadfast support of Casa Alterna—especially in these recent years, granting us access to an affordable home where hope and hospitality continue to meet friends at the threshold.

Love crosses borders—political borders, the borders we build in our hearts, and the border between this life and the next. Perfect love casts out fear, and on the other side awaits a more beautiful world.

With a debt of love and gratitude,
Anton

About the Author

Anton Flores-Maisonet is a writer, spiritual director, and co-founder of Casa Alterna, a community of radical hospitality with immigrants. Anton lives with his wife, Charlotte, at the Atlanta Friends Meeting, where he serves as Friend-in-Residence. His life and work are shaped by grief, grounded in faith, and sustained by a hope that welcomes—even in the hardest places. For more on Casa Alterna, visit casaalterna.org